Sowing

Atheism

Sowing Atheism

THE NATIONAL ACADEMY OF SCIENCES' SINISTER SCHEME TO TEACH OUR CHILDREN THEY'RE DESCENDED FROM REPTILES

Robert Bowie Johnson, Jr.

SOLVING LIGHT BOOKS

He is revealing the deep and concealed things;
Knowing what is in the darkness since with Him
A stream of light solves them.

Daniel 2:22

©2008 Robert Bowie Johnson, Jr.
Solving Light Books
727 Mount Alban Drive
Annapolis, MD 21409

SolvingLight.com

ISBN 978-0-9705438-5-1

Library of Congress Control Number: 2008902650

All Scripture passages, unless otherwise noted, are from the Concordant Translation, Concordant Publishing Concern, Santa Clarita, CA 91387 (Concordant.org).

Acknowledgements

Thanks to John Rothamel, Michael Thompson, Mark Wadsworth, Caroline Musterman, Jill Suing, Stella Stershic, John Anderson, Frank Bonarrigo, David Allen Deal, Pete Lounsbury, Ron Pramschufer, Nancy Beth Fisher, Lisa Marone, and Peggy Griggs.

Thanks also to AnswersinGenesis.org, CreationontheWeb.com, the Institute for Creation Research (icr.org), ScienceAgainstEvolution.org, and American Vision.

Special thanks to Dean H. Hough and James R. Coram, of *Unsearchable Riches*, a publication of the Concordant Publishing Concern, for their inspired and enlightening writings.

For Nancy Lee

TABLE OF CONTENTS

CHAPTER 1

The Atheists' Nest

The evolutionary transition from reptiles to mammals is particularly well-documented in the fossil record.

From the book *Science, Evolution, and Creationism* published by the National Academy of Sciences, 2008

Imagine yourself standing in the administrative offices of your local junior high school. You are there to bring a forgotten lunch to one of your children. Two tall, forbidding men enter wearing black business suits with red-letter NAS (National Academy of Sciences) armbands. They sneer and brush past you. They ignore the receptionist and the other people working there, and head straight for the principal's office. Just as the startled educator looks up at the intruders, both slam their fists on his desk. In unison, they cry, "We represent infallible science. You must teach these children that they are descended from reptiles. It is impossible to disprove our findings, and wrong to challenge them; therefore, no other point of view will be tolerated."

When these men disregard you again on their way out, you follow and yell down the hall, "What evidence do you have that we are descended from reptiles?" They reply, "We don't need any evidence. All we have to do is *say* we have it in abundance. We are the philosopher kings of science."

Like any parent, you'd be outraged at such a scare tactic, and fuming at such an inexcusable display of coercive arrogance on the part of what you had considered to be a respected American scientific organization. And you'd be even more incensed when you found out that the principal had caved into the browbeating and, just as the bullies demanded, ordered the science department to teach your children that they are, indeed, descended from reptiles.

But don't worry, those goons aren't going to march into your school any time soon. The National Academy of Sciences (NAS) has achieved the same result in another way—by promoting their new book, *Science, Evolution, and Creationism.* The book, published in January of 2008 in response to continuing challenges to Darwinism, targets "school board members, science teachers and other education leaders, policy makers, legal scholars, and others in the community who are committed to providing students with quality [reptile-based] science education" (my brackets). They sent a copy to every public school principal and every science teacher in America.

This NAS book is not about real science—an open-ended search for truth in nature and the cosmos. It is about promoting the philosophical and religious world-view of the NAS in the science classroom, and throughout the rest of the academic world, and ultimately, throughout our culture as a whole. It is about preventing any consideration, any mention in the science classroom, of a Creator or evidence for intelligent design in nature.

What exactly is the philosophical and religious world-view of the NAS? Atheism is their foundational belief. A survey conducted in 1998 by the science journal *Nature* of 517 members of the NAS, of which half replied, revealed that 7% believed in a "personal god," 20.8% expressed "doubt or agnosticism," and 72.2% expressed "personal disbelief."

The percent of outright atheists at the NAS is now even higher according to its own members. The following excerpt from the *Beyond Belief Conference* held in San Diego in November of 2006 is from Session Two, which began with a presentation from Neil deGrasse Tyson, the Director of the Hayden Planetarium, and one of the eighteen committee members responsible for producing the NAS book:

Tyson: I want to put on the table, not why 85% of the members of the National Academy of Sciences reject God, I want to know why 15% of the National Academy don't. That's really what we've got to address here. Otherwise, the public is secondary to this. [Moderator then turns to the panel for responses.]

Larry Krauss: It's hard to know how to respond to Neil, ever. But the question you asked about, "Why 15%," disturbs me a little bit because of this other presumption that scientists are somehow not people and that they don't have the same delusions—I mean, how many of them are pedophiles in the National Academy of Sciences? How many of them are Republicans? [laughter] And so, it would be amazing, of course, if it were zero. That would be the news story. But the point is I don't think you'd expect them, in general, to view their religion as a bulwark against science or to view the need to fly into buildings or whatever. So the delusions or predilections are important to recognize, that scientists are people and are as full of delusions about every aspect of their life as everyone else. We all make up inventions so that we can rationalize our existence and why we are who we are.

Tyson: But Lawrence, if you can't convert our colleagues, why do you have any hope that you're going to convert the public?

Note that Larry Krauss uses the word "delusions" three times as he refers to the beliefs of the 15% of the members of NAS who maintain some kind of faith in God; that is, those who are not outright atheists like the rest. In another part of his speech on this same subject, Tyson vehemently demands to know, "How come this number [the 15% who believe in God] isn't zero?" Tyson is quite correct to raise this question. He wants to know why all the members of NAS aren't atheists because logically, they should be. Atheism and evolutionary Darwinism are inextricably bound together. To maintain otherwise is to enter the realm of, as Krauss says, "delusions."

The serious Darwinists have always known this. Sir Julian Huxley, considered by some to be the primary architect of Neo-Darwinism, called evolution "religion without revelation." In 1964, Huxley wrote, "Evolution is the most powerful and the most comprehensive idea that has ever arisen on earth." Later in the same book he passionately argued that we must change "our pattern of religious thought from a God-centered to an evolution-centered pattern," going on to say that "the God hypothesis . . . is becoming an intellectual and moral burden on our thought." Therefore, he concluded that "we must construct something to take its place."[1]

As we'll see in Chapter 6, the NAS hierarchy, in order to bolster and "prove" its atheism, has constructed a closed, sacrosanct, counterfeit philosophy of science which completely eliminates the valid God hypothesis, along with any possibility of bringing it up again.

Atheists need a Godless science, and that's exactly what Darwinism gives them. Cornell University evolutionist Will Provine has acknowledged this obvious inference:

As the creationists claim, belief in modern evolution makes atheists of people. One can have a religious view that is compatible with evolution only if the religious view is indistinguishable from atheism.[2]

In his speech, part of which is cited on the previous page, Tyson referred to the members of the NAS as "the most brilliant minds the nation has." Such atheist elitism implies contempt for the non-elite, and it goes hand-in-hand with condescension towards those who worship the Supreme Spirit of Light and Love as their Creator and God.

Shortly after Neil Tyson spoke, Oxford professor and strident evolutionary atheist, Richard Dawkins, took the podium, heaping his usual scorn on all who believe in God. Dawkins entitled the first chapter of his latest book, *The God Delusion*, "A Deeply Religious Believer in No God." He is widely known for asserting that Darwinian evolution makes it possible to be an intellectually fulfilled atheist. His disdain for believers is total. He had asserted in the past:

It is absolutely safe to say that if you meet somebody who claims not to believe in evolution, that person is ignorant, stupid or insane (or wicked, but I'd rather not consider that).[3]

12

The literature of evolutionary atheism is rife with such contempt and condescension. Stephen Law wrote in 2002:

> **. . . the only way children can be taught that creationism is true and supported by the available evidence is by instilling in them such twisted conceptions of logic and evidential support that they are likely to remain gullible idiots for the rest of their lives.**
>
> **As I say, teaching that creationism is respectable science means teaching children to think in ways that are, literally, close to lunacy. [4]**

These are farmers of darkness, plowing into the minds of our children, planting their poisonous seeds of elitist atheistic evolution. Their deception is so systematized, so interwoven with bits of truth, that it is difficult for unwary readers to see with immediate clarity the false syllogism which animates the entire content of the NAS book:

All intelligent and competent scientists believe in evolution.
Creationists do not believe in evolution.
Therefore, creationists cannot be intelligent and competent scientists.

Science, Evolution, and Creationism is anything but an appeal to open-minded readers to use their powers of discernment to carefully consider the evidence. It is a cleverly disguised all-out, direct attack on the authority of the Word of God, and on all other challenges to their philosophical and religious dogma of evo-atheism (evolutionist atheism). In his speech, Tyson referred to himself and the other atheists of the NAS as "truth seekers." You'd think that these "truth seekers" would be somewhat forthcoming in their book about the institutional atheism at the NAS. But no, not a word, not an overt hint of the rank atheism governing every aspect of their examination of the natural world. The self-proclaimed elitist atheists in the hierarchy of the National Academy of Sciences know full-well that a candid presentation of their atheistic beliefs would only stir up resentment in America's Christian heartland. They can seek their atheistic "truth," they can even privately revel in it—they just can't be honest about it in a book designed to manipulate educators, teachers, and school children into it. And so in *Science, Evolution, and Creationism*, they expediently avow, for the benefit of gullible educators and teachers, that no conflict need exist between the Christian faith they despise and their brand of atheistic, evolutionary "science."

In Chapter 5, we'll examine this subterfuge in much detail because it is the most sinister part of their very sinister book. Let me give you a little foretaste of their deceitful hypocrisy now. The writers of the NAS book put forward the ruse that they are just thrilled that a few of their members embrace some kind of faith:

Many [evolutionary] scientists have written eloquently about how their [evolutionary] scientific studies have increased their awe and understanding of a creator. The study of [evolutionary] science need not lessen or compromise faith (my brackets). (p. 54).

Isn't that sweet! Come on in, everybody, especially you kids, and join the great evolutionary festivities! Learning about your descent by chance from worms and reptiles will strengthen your faith in "a creator," with a small "c," whoever he is.

But we've already seen the *true thoughts* that the members of the NAS hierarchy share with each other about those scientists who stubbornly retain some kind of faith in God:

I want to put on the table, not why 85% of the members of the National Academy of Sciences reject God, I want to know why 15% of the National Academy don't . . . How come this number isn't zero? (Neil deGrasse Tyson, from above).

In that same chapter, we'll see how the evo-atheists of the National Academy of Sciences conceal their rabid atheism behind a band of religious apostates who, having gutted and perverted the essential truths of Christianity, now act as willing shills for evo-atheistic propaganda. This is the black heart of their book.

14

We'll see in Chapter 7 that evo-atheism is fundamentally and intrinsically a belief-system, a religion—as opposed to genuine science. By insinuating their religion into public school science classrooms as the only approved belief-system in that environment, the NAS hierarchy violates the intent and spirit of the establishment clause of the First Amendment to the Constitution.

We'll see in Chapter 8 that the NAS violates the spirit and intent of the First Amendment in another way. Their book is an instrument structured to suppress free speech and free thought in the science classroom and beyond. We'll see that their technique fits a pattern of suppression with which you already may be familiar, and one with which I am very well-acquainted through personal experience with another powerful group of word- and thought-tyrants.

Nothing good can come from teaching our children they are descended from reptiles. Nothing. It is one of those things that is always all bad.

We had a character in our Chesapeake Bay community several years ago who was known for his deceitfulness. Among other fraudulent dealings, he'd sell unsuspecting souls a bushel of what he said were live, all-male blue crabs for what seemed like a good price. On the top, he'd put a layer of big crabs. But once a buyer got the bushel home and went through it, he or she would find female crabs underneath and, at the bottom of the bushel, many illegal (too small) males. Sometimes, half the crabs would be dead and unsteamable. People called this character "the weasel."

In *Science, Evolution, and Creationism*, the NAS offers us several bushel baskets of what they say are evidence for evolution. But once we get past the top layer of rhetoric and go through the rest of the bushel piece by piece, as we do in Chapter 3 of this book, we find no actual evidence *at all* for the notion that we are descended from reptiles. When we look carefully, we find that the weasels from the NAS have presented us with bushel baskets empty of evidence. You may say here that I am name-calling. I most decidedly am not. What do you call people with a hidden, shameless agenda who try to sell you

15

something that's not really there—who try to *sell something to your children* that's not really there—if not weasels?

When my daughter, Beth, reviewed my first draft of the manuscript for this book, she pointed out that the NAS book writers are worse than weasels. "They are more like termites," she said, "because with termites, you don't see the damage, you don't notice how thoroughly the truth has been undermined until it's too late."

The evo-atheists have fabricated what they call an "evolutionary tree." They maintain that any two living species today can be traced back to a common ancestor on their tree. According to their speculation therefore, a weasel and a termite can be traced back to the same ancestor. This is the fossil the geniuses at the NAS should be out in the field digging for. They are its first cousins.

Once we have established in Chapter 3 that the evo-atheists cannot produce any actual evidence for the origin of life, for the emergence of the sexes, or for the evolution of one distinct kind of organism into another, we go on in Chapter 4 to explain how, then, they and their "theory" are able to dominate the minds of so many. The answer is categorically and emphatically: seduction and deception.

Atheism thrives in academia. In Chapter 6, we're going to search out the origins of academia in the philosophy of the ancient academy of Plato in Athens, and learn how it connects to the NAS's seduction and deceit. We'll see that the philosophy which animates their atheistic religion came through the mind of Plato's mouthpiece, Sokrates, a totalitarian, elitist snob.

In Chapter 9, I present my own documented theory of the meaning of ancient Greek art, including the meaning of the sculptures of the Parthenon, and those of the temple of Zeus at Olympia. I maintain that the record shows that the Greeks have left us an account of their origins which matches in convincing detail the key events described in Genesis. If my theory is true, it completely confounds the tenets of atheistic evolution from an unexpected direction. But please, examine my evidence and judge for yourself.

Jesus said that it is not what goes into a man that defiles him, but rather, what comes out of a man. What has come out of the leadership of the NAS most recently is *Science, Evolution, and Creationism*, a book which demands that the atheistic religious philosophy embraced by its hierarchy be taught exclusively and unchallenged in every public school science classroom in America. The evo-atheists attempt to disguise their true motives, but the very words and phrases they use in their book expose and defeat their own abominable purpose. They try to hide their atheism, but their associates betray them. They try to hide their lack of evidence, but their own language gives them away. They try to destroy creationism, but it emerges stronger than ever. They try to misrepresent Bible-believing Christians, but their scheme backfires. They try to use enchantment to overcome their lack of truth, but it winds up ensnaring them instead. Their book thus becomes a tad more "educational" than they had intended.

I love the English language and what it can reveal. In their preface (p. xii)—right from the get-go, so to speak—the NAS writers unconsciously concede that their evo-atheist viewpoint is false. They write that their booklet "shows how evolutionary theory *reflects* the nature of science" (my emphasis). A reflection does not produce a true picture. When you look in the mirror, your right eye becomes your left eye; your right arm becomes your left arm, etc. A reflection produces a false image, a backwards image. The NAS writers are quite correct: their "evolutionary theory" does, in fact, reflect "the nature of science;" that is, their "evolutionary theory" gets "the nature of science" exactly backwards. Their own words are thus the very thesis of this book.

Whether you've looked into the issues dealt with here in any depth or not, you are in for some more exciting surprises in the chapters that follow.

17

Chapter 2

THE THEFT OF TRUE SCIENCE

The thief is not coming except that he should be stealing and sacrificing and destroying.

John 10:10

Here is my definition of science:

Science is the systematic, unbiased examination of nature and the cosmos, the formulation of the truths found thereby into general laws, and their application for humanitarian, political, and economic purposes.

The "unbiased examination of nature and the cosmos" is, in effect, the search for truth. Our attitude towards science should ever be one of inquiry. A scientist's task is to ascertain what a thing *does* mean. He or she must not presume to dictate what it *must* mean. Such a predisposition demonstrates bias. A scientific teaching must rest on positive, unquestioned statement of fact, not on gratuitous assumptions or specious arguments.

In accord with my definition of science, we try to the best of our ability to let nature and the cosmos speak for themselves. In regard to what is happening on this earth, we try to let the structure and events of nature lead us where they will.

Neither belief in creationism nor evolution is necessary to the actual examination of nature itself. Creationists look at the Grand Canyon and see the result of the upheavals caused by Noah's Flood. The evo-atheists look at the Grand Canyon and see millions of years of erosion. The evidence for both interpretations is exactly the same. On page 26 of their book, the NAS authors write, "The bones in the forelimbs of terrestrial and some aquatic vertebrates are remarkably similar because they have all evolved from the forelimbs of a common ancestor." A creationist, examining the same evidence would say that the similarity is a result of the fact that all these vertebrates were made by the same Creator. To the ones examining the vertebrates, what difference does it make? None.

Evidence is not the problem: it is the interpretation that causes the controversy. Creationism and evolution both interpret the structure and events of nature, representing opposite hypotheses with different assumptions. The creation hypothesis, or the God hypothesis, looks at the apparent design in nature, and says that this points to a Creator. The evolutionary hypothesis also sees the apparent design in nature, but says that this is illusory, and that all life can be explained chemically and materialistically (methodological materialism) without reference to a Creator.

An honest scientist cannot exclude either explanation of nature without presenting evidence for that exclusion. Is it possible that there *is* a Creator God? Is it possible that there *is not* a Creator God? The answer to both questions is "Yes." When we muster as much "objectivity" as we humans are able, we have to answer both of these questions in the affirmative. Unbiased science accepts the reality of both of these possible explanations for existence. Arbitrarily excluding one of these explanations in our search for truth is fundamentally unscientific; that is, it is the abandonment of the "open-ended search-for-truth" frame of mind *in favor of* something else.

A scientist ought to behave like a detective in that they both have to search for clues and further information leading to a conclusion. Just about half the shows on evening television concern police investigations. From Miss Marple to Joe Friday to Horatio Kane, we're all familiar with the logic of the investigative process. In a murder investigation, would detective Eddie Green of *Law and Order* exclude a possible suspect without grounds for that exclusion? Of course not. If he did, the whole police investigative process would not make sense to us, and it would suggest some degree of prejudice on his part. That's why fictional detectives and real detectives always insist upon evidence (e.g., an alibi which proves non-involvement) before they exclude a person as a suspect.

A bad situation only gets worse if, in addition to arbitrarily excluding one suspect, detectives railroad someone else out of a predisposed desire to see them punished, regardless of the evidence.

In the same way, the investigative procedures of true science do not make sense if they arbitrarily exclude one possible explanation for phenomena *in favor of* another. There is a genuine possibility that there is a Creator God, and that therefore, nature is designed. Absent any proof otherwise, the God hypothesis remains a valid scientific hypothesis.

ARBITRARILY EXCLUDING THE GOD HYPOTHESIS

We saw in Chapter 1 that, in 1964, Julian Huxley urged his fellow evo-atheists to construct something to replace the intellectually and morally burdensome (to them) God hypothesis.

Science, Evolution, and Creationism, the book published by the atheistic hierarchy at the NAS, has given us a summary of that "something" which, in response to Huxley's order, they have fabricated—not only to take the place of the God hypothesis, but to obliterate its mention from America's public school science classrooms. The NAS's arbitrary exclusion of the God hypothesis leaves only one possible explanation for our existence—their atheistic evolutionary one. There is now only one brand of science available, a brand they insist that everyone—from kindergarten children to laboratory researchers—must be satisfied with.

Their arbitrary exclusion of the valid God hypothesis is based entirely on their atheistic prejudices, the world-view they *favor*, and not upon sound scientific principles. All investigations of nature ought to be *un*branded, or generic, in the sense of being nonspecific insofar as the God hypothesis and the evolution hypothesis are concerned. Ideally, let unbiased researchers present their findings from their systematic examinations of nature, and let the creationists and atheists interpret the findings in terms of their respective assumptions, or hypotheses. The interpretation of the findings (the evidence) that makes the most sense is the one more qualified to a "theory" status.

The atheists at the NAS cannot allow the open competition of the two hypotheses, because based on what we actually see in nature, the God hypothesis always makes more sense. To get around that severe problem, the NAS must, by atheistic fiat, brand all science as exclusively evolutionary. Science becomes "evolutionary science." Biology becomes "evolutionary biology." Anthropology becomes "evolutionary anthropology." Their goal is to force-feed you and your children their atheistic brand, and their atheistic brand only. Are your kids hungry for information on the origins and purpose of humanity? Do they wonder how they got here? Fix them another bowl of evo-atheism. That's all that's left on the shelf.

STAINING NATURE THE COLOR OF ATHEISM

Let me give you a more vivid explanation of what has happened in our public school science classrooms. The evo-atheists of the NAS see nature *only* through their gray atheist goggles. These dogmatists see all living flora and fauna, all microscopic cells, and all fossils the same way—as saturated with that drab color. They don't want our children to see the glorious yellows, oranges, greens, purples, and blues of nature, but they cannot force them to put on their gray atheist goggles as they enter the classroom. Instead, to achieve the same effect, they stain all of nature dark gray, so that the kids see *only* what the evo-atheists do. The evo-atheists insist that all students accept the dark gray stain as normal when, in fact, it is artificial, and philosophically and religiously generated.

How do they stain all of nature with their dark gray atheist color? We'll see in the beginning of Chapter 4 that the NAS book writers repeat the idea that "evolution is true, and all scientists believe it" in slightly different words over 80 times in their book, a book with only 55 pages of text. With each repetition, the gray gets darker and darker.

The NAS writers also say, without providing the evidence for it, that "evolution is science," and they insist throughout that evolution is not only a valid theory but a "fact" as well. They claim that scientists no longer question whether evolution occurred but only how (dark gray) evolution occurred.

At the direction of the NAS, the National Association of Biology Teachers dons the gray goggles and, on behalf of the NAS, stains nature the dark gray atheist color. Here is their explanation of life's origins that they adopted in 1995:

The diversity of life on earth is the outcome of evolution: an unsupervised, impersonal, unpredictable and natural process of temporal descent with genetic modification that is affected by natural selection, chance, historical contingencies and changing environments.

The pseudo-scientists of the NAS do not investigate to determine what a particular thing in nature *is*. Their gray stain on all of nature tells them what a particular thing *must* be—always "evidence" for evolution, and by extension, for atheism. Science is no longer "the systematic, unbiased examination of nature and the cosmos." It has become "the interpretation of nature through the gray lens of atheism, and the tainting of all natural phenomena with that gray stain."

THE GOD HYPOTHESIS IS SCIENCE, NOT RELIGION

The atheistic hierarchy at the NAS denies the God hypothesis. It threatens their world-view—it is the *only* threat to their world-view—so they must keep it out of the science classroom. The question is, how, without producing any evidence for its exclusion, do they convince others to dismiss the God hypothesis? They call it religion, and say religion has no place in science. The God hypothesis is no more a religion than is our national motto, "In God We Trust." Thomas Jefferson wrote in our Declaration of Independence:

We hold these truths to be self-evident, that all men are created equal, that they are endowed by their Creator with certain unalienable Rights, that among these are Life, Liberty and the pursuit of Happiness.

The unadorned acknowledgement of the Creator God is not religion, and never has been. If the recognition of our Creator in our founding political document is not religion, then merely hypothesizing the existence of a Creator in science cannot possibly be religion. Again, the God hypothesis is a valid explanation for the structure and events of nature—an explanation detested by the atheists who rule the National Academy of Sciences.

Creationists do not want to bring religion into the classroom. With all the different sects of Christianity, some of them very strange, and all the other Creator-acknowledging religions, that would lead to chaos. Creationists simply want the God hypothesis brought back into the science classroom, and recognized for what it is—a scientifically valid hypothesis. We'll see in Chapter 7 that, beyond question, it is the hierarchy of NAS which is forcing religion—its brand of atheistic religion—into the science classroom.

EVOLUTION ACCORDING TO THE NAS

What, exactly, according to the National Academy of Sciences, is evolution? Its book does not contain a quotable definition of it, but given what is avowed throughout, it defines evolution in this way:

Evolution is a proven theory and a fact, which explains how, from a single-celled, chemically generated, life form, the diversity of life, including humanity, came into being over several billion years through an undirected process of random mutations acted upon by natural selection.

What is a random mutation? Random means "unpredictable," while a mutation is a variation from the norm—the very definition of "aberration." Check your own dictionaries. Thus, random mutations are

24

unpredictable aberrations. The NAS book equates these unpredictable aberrations with genetic copying mistakes.

The NAS book also identifies natural selection as "the driving force behind evolution" (p. 23), but it does not specify what kind of "force" it is. For example, is it measured as genuine forces would be, in dynes or newtons? A force is a push or a pull upon an object which results from its interaction with another object. What exactly are the objects which are interacting? Are they being pushed or pulled? Is the driving force mechanical, gravitational, electrical, or magnetic? The NAS book remains silent on these points.

Newton's Third Law, formally stated, is "For every action, there is an equal and opposite reaction." What is the equal and opposite reaction to natural selection, "the driving force behind evolution"? Again, the NAS book is silent.

Another section of the NAS book says something quite different about natural selection:

The differential reproductive success of organisms with advantageous traits is known as *natural selection*, because nature "selects" traits that enhance the ability of organisms to survive and reproduce (emphasis in original). (p. 5).

In this passage, it is not a force at all, but an outcome or result ("reproductive success") of some kind of ill-defined actions. On page 50, they also define natural selection as a "process." Is natural selection, the key concept of Darwinian evolution, a force, a process, or an outcome? In reality, it is none of the three. And so, what is it then? We find the essential clue in the above-cited sentence.

Note that the NAS writers have put the word "selects" in quotes. They do this because they know there is no actual selecting going on. Nature is not a conscious being with a will. Nature cannot and does not literally "select" anything. The term "natural selection" is not literal at all; it is figurative. Natural selection is not a real force, a real process, or a real result of anything. It is nothing more than a figure of speech. Natural "selection" falls under the category of metaphor in that it is an implied comparison of two unlike things (a human and what he or she can do, and all of nature), and it falls more specifically under the category of personification in that it applies human qualities to natural phenomena—nature itself in this case. Unable to describe the evolutionary origin of the species in scientific terms, the members of the NAS, as Darwin before them, resort to an elusive literary device. In a letter to a friend, Darwin referred to natural selection as a "she."[1]

Darwin also referred to natural selection as "survival of the fittest," another extremely problematic phrase for today's evo-atheists. The NAS writers don't use the phrase at all in their book. One reason is that racists like Hitler used the term to justify their evil. Another reason they don't use the phrase is that it is a tautology.

Tautology comes from a Greek word which means "redundant." An obvious tautology is "bachelors are unmarried." This statement conveys no real information because, by definition, a bachelor is someone who is unmarried. Those who are unfit to survive do not survive. Survival of the fittest is thus nothing more than the survival of those who survive. The Darwinian term "survival of the fittest" conveys no useful information to us. We already know that the survivors survived.

So how did we humans, according to the NAS book, come into being here, on planet earth? All living things, including us, can be traced back approximately two billion years to a first single-celled organism. (As we shall see in the next chapter, the evolutionists have no explanation whatever for how this first cell came into being). Nevertheless, this cell supposedly reproduced and eventually formed a population of similar cells. Then genetic mistakes began to occur, due to radiation or some other unknown cause. Some of these genetic mistakes (unpredictable aberrations or random mutations) had a negative effect on the organisms' reproductive fitness, some had no effect, but yet some "enhanced" the ability of these organisms to survive and reproduce.

Then, natural "selection," an unquantifiable "force" and/or very sketchy "process" or "result," that meets the definition of a figure of speech, got involved, causing a new, more complex population of organisms—a different species—to appear. This same figure of speech, known as natural "selection," continued to operate in some way upon ever greater numbers of genetic copying errors (unpredictable aberrations), and more and more species came into being until life reached the stage of complexity that plants and animals emerged. Eventually, over a period of about 250 million years (that's 250 million earth-trips around the sun), we humans evolved from reptiles, by the same process—a figure of speech operating upon the genetic copying errors of reproductive cells.

The evo-atheists of the NAS claim this above-described evolution of theirs is a "fact," yet they have been unable to formulate a "law of evolution," or a "law of natural selection," or a "law of random mutations." I sympathize with their inabilities. How does one formulate into a law something that's really nothing more than a dark gray atheistic stain upon nature?

We've seen now what evolution means to the evo-atheists at the NAS. What to them is science? We will see in the next six chapters that what they write in their own book demonstrates that their "understanding" of science turns out to be nothing more than the manipulation of language and atheistically-stained evidence to prove that evolution is true, and thus that God does not exist. Their arbitrary staining, or tainting, of all nature with their atheism is an important part of their "scientific method." The hierarchy of the NAS has stolen true science; they are sacrificing our children to their atheism, and at the same time, destroying our children's faith in God.

CHAPTER 3

Philosophy and Empty Seduction: The Emptiness

Beware that no one shall be despoiling you through philosophy and empty seduction, in accord with human tradition, in accord with the elements of the world, and not in accord with Christ, for in Him the entire complement of the Deity is dwelling bodily (Colossians 2:8-9).

The above verses from Colossians present us with a stark contrast between the truth that is said to be in Christ and the falsehoods allegedly embraced by the evo-atheists. The verses define the things that lead to the kind of human thinking which purports to contradict the truth in Christ and in the Scriptures, and we are warned to beware of them. These things include "philosophy and empty seduction."

Evo-atheism utterly contradicts the idea that the truth of humanity's origin and purpose is found in Christ and in the Scriptures as a whole. Now, if the passage cited above from Colossians is true, then we ought to easily be able to show that Darwinism as a theory is nothing but philosophy and empty seduction. A theory that is not empty, or not void of evidence and merit, does not need seduction to sustain it. So we're going to start with the "empty" part, then in the next two chapters, discuss the seduction surrounding the great void in evo-atheism. Philosophy—from the Greek *philo-sophia*, fondness for human wisdom and reasoning—is a more complicated subject, involving as it does a systematizing of the seduction and the concomitant deception. So we will devote all of Chapter 6 to philosophy and its rule over the hierarchy of the National Academy of Sciences, and over all others who embrace the notion we evolved by chance over millions of years through and from reptiles.

In order to sustain a valid theory of the evolution of the species by chance from inert matter, proponents of it need to provide evidence for three things: first, they need to show how the inert matter became alive;

29

second, they need evidence of how the sexes evolved; and third, they need to show, step by step, how an organism, any living organism, evolved from five or so of its predecessor species, step by step. That alleged process is called speciation.

To see how much evidence the NAS has for these things, let's picture three mason jars next to each other on a table. No, mason jars are too small. Again and again, the NAS book writers claim that the evidence for evolution is "overwhelming." We don't want evidence spilling out all over the floor, so we'll use metal bushel baskets to contain it all. Let's picture ourselves, then, taking the evidence from the evo-atheists as they offer it, and dropping it, piece by piece, into the respective bushel baskets.

THE FIRST BUSHEL BASKET

Let's see how much evidence we can drop in the first basket. The authors of the NAS book admit that they can produce no evidence whatsoever showing that inert matter, by chance, turned into an information-based life form, writing, "Constructing a plausible hypothesis of life's origins will require that many questions be answered" (p. 22). Let me emphasize that this is an explicit acknowledgement from the NAS that not only do they have no evidence for the origin of life, but they also have no "plausible hypothesis" for it either. The first basket must thus remain empty.

It is important to note that without any evidence at all for it, they still insist that life began by a chance occurrence: matter suddenly turned into a living cell capable of reproducing itself, and "evolving" over billions of years into the millions of different kinds of life on earth today. They cannot describe what specifically happened, how it happened, where it happened, why it happened, or when it happened, yet they adamantly maintain that it happened.

If a man kept showing up at the police station, insisting that a crime had occurred, but could not say specifically what had happened, or how, where, why, or when it happened, he'd be charged with filing a false report. Darwinism is, and always has been, a false report. Its evidence-lacking insistence on this point is just a small part of what makes Darwinism a philosophy of science, and not science itself.

THE SECOND BUSHEL BASKET

Now for the second bushel basket. Mark 10:6 tells us creationists that "from the beginning of creation God makes them male and female." The evolutionists say that the sexes evolved over hundreds of millions of years through genetic copying errors acted upon by that elusive figure of speech, natural selection. What evidence do they have for the evolution of the sexes? They just might have some, because I'm looking at an article in *The Washington Post* by David Brown about genomes, chimpanzees, and mankind wherein he asserts as facts that "scientists have confirmed how sex evolved," and that our X and Y chromosomes "are descended from the same 'ancestor chromosome' which existed 300 million years ago at the dawn of this form of sexual reproduction." Before we drop these facts into the second bushel basket, all we have to do is find out where he got them, and verify them.

It turns out that Brown found these facts in another article written in *The Washington Post* six months earlier (March 17, 2005, page A3) by reporter Rick Weiss. Weiss is reporting on an article that appeared in *Nature* magazine. The headline reads, "Human X Chromosome Coded," and the subhead line reads: "Sequence Confirms How Sex Evolved and Explains Some Male-Female Differences." Note the word "Confirms." To confirm means "to give new assurance of the truth of; verify; corroborate." Is this the verification we're looking for? Sorry, no. Despite the promising subhead line, Weiss presents no evidence at all in the text of the article confirming how sex evolved (neither did his source, *Nature* magazine)—just these two utterly speculative sentences:

It happened about 300 million years ago, long before the first mammals. A conventional chromosome in a forebear of humans—

31

probably a reptile of some sort—apparently underwent a mutation that allowed it to direct the development of sperm-producing testes.

Does "Probably a reptile of some sort [which] apparently underwent a mutation" qualify as evidence? No, we really cannot put that into the second bushel basket as a fact. *The Washington Post* has editorialized that the evidence for evolution is "overwhelming" and "powerful." How can such a prestigious newspaper allow such idiotic speculation to pass for proof? They do it all the time, as do hundreds of other mainstream newspapers and magazines who also "believe" in evolution. They have no evidence for how the sexes evolved, so they try to fill up the basket with "Probably a reptile of some sort [which] apparently underwent a mutation" type of stuff. Our evidence basket is no place for make-believe events, or for that matter, any other sham "evidence" they have concocted. The NAS has no evidence for how the sexes allegedly evolved. Alas, the second bushel basket must remain empty.

Our endeavor to find the evidence, however, has been instructive, for we have learned how evo-atheists try to fake "evolutionary" evidence for the origins of male and female. How many readers just skimming the article, including school-children, trusted *The Washington Post* and its reporter to be honest, and were thus enticed by the false subhead line to believe that scientists actually possess confirmed evidence for the evolutionary origin of the sexes?

The Washington Post article also gives us insight into an aspect of the evolutionists' true "scientific method"—transmuting speculation into fact just by saying it is so. And don't kid yourself—it's not just this bushel basket they try to force counterfeit evidence into—it is all three.

THE THIRD BUSHEL BASKET

The third bushel basket is the place reserved for us to put evidence of speciation, as the NAS defines it, "The evolutionary processes through which new species arise from existing species." Earlier, I referred to the need to take one specific species back through its immediate predecessor species, and through the one before that, etc., ultimately yielding a clear line of unbroken related descent going back to the fifth ancestor species, with each of the species being unambiguously identified. But since the effort of the NAS to fill the other baskets has been so abysmal, we are going to cut them some slack with this basket. All we are going to ask is that they provide just the one immediate ancestor-species of any existing species. With all their boasting, that should be a snap for the NAS book writers. They write the following on page 24 of their book:

Each species that lives on Earth today is the product of an evolutionary lineage—that is, it arose from a preexisting species, which itself arose from a preexisting species, and so on back through time.

This is written in the indicative mood, the mood of fact, and it is written with great confidence. We should expect then, to be told specifically what species preceded us. The NAS book says on the same page, ". . . humans are not descended from chimpanzees or from any other ape living today but from a species that no longer exists." Do the NAS writers identify that species? If they do, we've got some potential evidence for the third bushel basket. But alas, no, the NAS book does not identify the specific species from which we supposedly evolved. What we have here is nothing but an unfounded assertion of speciation, and nothing else. We cannot put this in the evidence basket.

The NAS writers don't know the identity of our immediate pre-existing species, so I guess there is no point in asking them to identify the pre-existing species from which our immediate pre-existing species "evolved." And there is surely no sense in repeating that fruitless and empty process "so on back through time."

This patently ludicrous scenario reminds me of the newly-hired piccolo player joke. On his first day in church, he can't play any of the hymns. When the preacher turns his back on the congregation, a person stands up and says "the piccolo player is an idiot," and sits back down. The preacher returns to the pulpit and demands that the person who said that stand up. When the person doesn't stand up, the preacher asks the person sitting next to the person who called the piccolo player an idiot to stand up. When that person doesn't stand up, he asks the person sitting next to the person, sitting next to the person . . . etc. (In such a proper Sunday morning setting such as that, time can only ooze sluggishly).

After it is taken to the tenth degree, or as far as the joke audience will allow, someone stands up in the back and says, "I am not the person sitting next to the person, sitting next to the person, sitting next to the person," etc., going back through the whole sequence, one at a time, until he finally gets to: "And I am not the person who called the piccolo player an idiot, but," he continues, "what I and the rest of the people in this congregation want to know is: who called that idiot a piccolo player?"

It is about time that, in our public school and college science classes, some students who see the real truth and the real issues, begin standing up in the back of the class, demanding of their teachers, "Who called that evolutionary speculation evidence?"

CONFUSION PORTRAYED AS EVIDENCE

The cover of the October 9, 2006 *Time Magazine* featured a chimp's face juxtaposed next to a human baby's face. Between them appeared the words, "How We Became Human. Chimps and humans share almost 99% of their DNA. New discoveries reveal how we can be so alike—and yet so different." The reporters, Michael D. Lemonick and Andrea Dorfman wrote the article as if evolution were an absolutely proven fact. The main logical error they embrace is the idea that similar DNA in two species means that the most advanced species evolved from the other. A better explanation for the similarity is that the same Creator made humans, chimps, and every other living thing, but with such article sources as the Max Planck Institute for Evolutionary Biology, the God hypothesis is forbidden.

34

The *Time* article points out that 3 billion is the number of base pairs in the human genome, *only* 1.23% of which are different in the chimp genome. Suddenly, I want to eat a banana and swing through the trees! Let's multiply that 1.23% times 3 billion (something the article writers don't do for us): it comes to 36,900,000 different base pairs that, according to their beliefs, are the result of 36,900,000 unpredictable aberrations, or genetic copying mistakes. Remember, these represent only the so-called "beneficial" copying errors. To get these 36,900,000 good errors (if that phrase makes sense), there had to have occurred hundreds of millions, or even thousands of millions of neutral and harmful copying mistakes. How does a species which endures hundreds of millions of harmful genetic copying errors—the kind that lead to disease and deformity—survive, much less progress?

The *Time* article went into some detail about the most unusual findings of David Reich of the Broad Institute, whose founding director is a member of the NAS:

Reich's team measured how the evolutionary clock varied across chromosomes in the different species. To their surprise, they *deduced* that chimps and humans split from a common ancestor no more than 6.3 million years ago and *probably* less than 5.4 million years ago. *If* they're correct, several hominid species *now considered* to be among our earliest ancestors—Sahelanthropus tchadensis (7 million years old), Orrorin tugenenesis (about 6 million years old) and Ardipithecus kadabba (5.2 to 5.7 million years old)—*may have to be re-evaluated*.

And that's not the most startling finding. Reich's team also found the entire human X chromosome diverged from the chimp's X chromosome about 1.2 million years later than the other chromosomes. One *plausible explanation* is that chimps and humans first split but later interbred from time to time before finally going their separate evolutionary ways. That *could explain* why some of the most ancient fossils now considered human ancestors have such striking mixtures of chimp and human traits—some *could actually have been* hybrids. Or *they might have* simply coexisted with, or even predated, the last common ancestor of chimps and humans (my emphases).

What are "scientist" Reich and the two reporters who wrote this article doing here? They are fabricating and fondling falsehood, plain and simple. Note that, at the end of the first paragraph, what used to pass for evidence now "may have to be re-evaluated." The "evidence" for evolution always needs to be re-evaluated because there is never any substance to it.

You would think that in an 86-page book, the NAS could present ten or twenty pages of straightforward evidence for evolution, explaining how hearing and eyesight developed among animals, how insects and birds grew wings and learned to fly, how the spider learned its weaving craft, how ants and bees learned to socialize, and how a blade of grass became a redwood tree—all through a series of millions of unpredictable aberrations. The NAS book authors refer to an "immense body of evidence" proving evolution, but yet neglect to give us any details about said evidence.

EVOLUTION IS ALWAYS ASSUMED, NEVER PROVEN

The NAS book claims on page 23 that:

In the more recent fossil record, the evolutionary paths of many modern organisms, such as whales, elephants, armadillos, horses and humans have been uncovered.

We've seen that the human "evolutionary path" is about as unspecific as it can be. What about horses? Can the evo-atheists present any evidence for their speciation? They say they can. The typical fossil display includes four horse skeletons in line, ordered from the smallest to the largest, implying that over millions of years, that's how they evolved. Before we get into more detail on the horses, let me share a quote from atheist NAS spokesman Neil deGrasse Tyson. It is from his speech during Session Two of the *Beyond Belief Conference* held in San Diego in November of 2006:

At our museum in New York, the American Museum of Natural History, they [Bible-believing Christians] come to the Big Bang exhibit and sometimes I don't feel like having that conversation. I say, "Why don't you go to our hall of human biology first and then come to us." And that's where we have sort of monkeys holding hands with people in skeleton forms and then they [the Bible-believing Christians] never make it back to the Big Bang. They're gone forever, okay. So however egregious the Big Bang is [to them], monkeys and people is a worse transgression, apparently (laughter).

Please note first Tyson's ridicule of Bible-believing Christians. And second, note that Tyson and his pals at the museum have set up monkeys and people holding hands. No thinking person would mistake this kind of a set-up for evidence of evolution. It does show, however, their propensity to create displays in such a way so as to make visitors think that people and monkeys share a common ancestor who sits on an imaginary branch of their whimsical evolutionary tree. The horse displays amount to essentially the same kind of set-up.

Writer Peter Hastie has debunked the idea of proof for horse evolution making, among many others, the following key points:

We ought to find the earliest horse fossils in the lowest rock strata, but we don't. The so-called "earliest" horses have been found near the surface, sometimes right next to modern horse fossils. The fossil fragments have been gathered from several continents on the assumption of evolutionary progress, and then used to support the assumption.

"When evolutionists assume that the horse has grown progressively in size over millions of years," Mr. Hastie writes, "what they forget is that modern horses vary enormously in size. The largest horse today is the Clydesdale; the smallest is the Fallabella, which stands at 17 inches (43 centimeters) tall. Both are members of the same species, and neither has evolved from the other."[1]

Finally, Mr. Hastie quotes evolutionist Dr. Niles Eldredge, curator of the American Museum of Natural History:

I admit that an awful lot of that (imaginary stories) has gotten into the textbooks as though it were true. For instance, the most famous example still on exhibit downstairs (in the American Museum) is the exhibit on horse evolution prepared perhaps 50 years ago. That has been presented as literal truth in textbook after textbook. Now I think that that is lamentable . . . [2]

When pressed, the evo-atheists admit they have no evidence for horse speciation. What about the whales, elephants, and armadillos they mention? The NAS writers present no evidence for their speciation. I searched evolution-friendly Web sites but was unable to find the identity of any of their direct ancestors. I invite you to go on the Internet yourself to find the proof we're looking for. Good luck. I was able to retrieve the following information from some of those sites: "The direct ancestor to the modern-day elephant is unknown . . .," "Some details (about the whale) remain fuzzy and under investigation," and "There isn't much information on the evolution of the nine-banded armadillo."

The NAS book devotes two pages to a fossil uncovered in northern Canada they named *Tiktaalik* from the Inuit word for "big freshwater fish." They claim it represents a 375-million-year-old missing link between water and land animals. They refuse any challenges to their dating methods. For their evolutionary speculation to be true, these fossils *have to be* that old. The cataclysmic upheavels of Noah's Flood are what most likely trapped Tiktaalik. The NAS writers say that the most important thing is that "its fins contained bones that formed a limb-like appendage that the animal could use to move and prop itself up" (p. 3). Creation scientists have already shown that the Tiktaalik's fin was not connected to the main skeleton, so could not have supported its weight on land.

It won't be long before Tiktaalik has gone through the typical "missing link" life cycle: fragments found, imaginative interpretation, popular publication, data dismissed. Remember the distorted skull and jaw fragments of the "Chad Ape-Man?" *The Washington Post* editors made a huge deal over it. The July 11, 2002, issue of *Nature* wrote about it:

This skull's combination of primitive and advanced features suggests remarkable past diversity in the human family tree, and should ensure that the term 'missing link' is consigned to history.

Only three months later, other scientists writing in the October 10, 2002, issue of *Nature*, who went into more detail, discredited the find as just another ape—a record time for the completion of the "fragments found" to "data dismissed" cycle. [3]

Tiktaalik is really irrelevant to our effort to put evidence of speciation into the third bushel basket because the evo-atheists cannot identify the species from which, or into which, Tiktaalik allegedly evolved.

Neil Shubin, the paleontologist who found Tiktaalik in 2004, has written a book entitled, *Your Inner Fish: A Journey into the 3.5-Billion-Year History of the Human Body*. Evo-atheist professor of biological anthropology, Barbara J. King, reviewed it in the February 17-23, 2008 edition of *The Washington Post Book World*. King reported that "Shubin wants us to see our history not only as primates, but also as insects and worms."

Please keep the insects and worms in your family, Shubin. Some of us were created as spiritual beings, in the image of our Creator.

The *Book World* editors entitled the review "The Missing Link," without the quotes. This demonstrates just how eager papers such as *The Washington Post* are to present evo-atheist speculation as fact. I can see giving a doctoral candidate an extra few months to complete his or her thesis. But giving the evo-atheists 150 years to produce a genuine missing link is a bit too lenient.

The NAS writers also reference a bird fossil called *Archaeopteryx* they claim is 155 million-years-old, and try to make a feathered dinosaur out of it. But Dr. Alan Feduccia, a world authority on birds at the University of North Carolina at Chapel Hill, and an evolutionist himself, discounts their speculation:

39

Paleontologists have tried to turn *Archaeopteryx* into an earth-bound, feathered dinosaur. But it's not. It is a bird, a perching bird. And no amount of 'paleobabble' is going to change that.[4]

And as with Tiktaalik, the evo-atheists cannot identify the species from which, or into which, Archaeopteryx allegedly evolved. So, we still have no evidence of speciation to put into our third bushel basket.

On page 23, in between their mention of Tiktaalik and their mention of Archaeopteryx, the NAS writers sandwich in these two sentences:

Fossils from about 330 million years ago *document* the evolution of large amphibians from the early tetrapods [animals with four legs]. Well-preserved skeletons from rocks that are 230 million years old *show* dinosaurs evolving from a lineage of reptiles (my emphases).

Think about this: the NAS writers go into detail about two fossils for which they cannot demonstrate speciation. Yet, they give no details and present no images for fossils they claim "document" and "show" speciation. If, as they claim, these fossils did, in fact, document and show speciation, they would have put their evidence on the front cover of their book. The evo-atheists cannot name the direct ancestor species of any living species, and yet they expect us to believe they've got the scoop on species they say lived hundreds of millions of years ago. They do not have any evidence at all for speciation. In the above passage, they are trying to sneak by the unwary reader a false claim for it. Again, they are not interested in uncovering the truths of nature; they want to justify their atheism. At any rate, false claims don't cut it. We are looking for evidence for speciation, and the NAS does not have any. The third bushel basket must remain empty.

The NAS book is the product of a large committee. You know the old saying, "Too many atheists spoil the pretense." On page 52, one of their writers basically admits they have no evidence for the origin of sex or speciation with this phrase: "Of course, there remain many interesting questions about evolution, such as the evolutionary origin of sex or different mechanisms of speciation . . ." How about demonstrating just one mechanism of speciation for just one species? A clam, a potato, a grasshopper, a slug, a tulip, an anchovy, anything!

Three empty bushel baskets sitting in a row. "Evolution evidence for sale! Evolution evidence for sale! Get your bushel-baskets-full right here at the NAS headquarters!" Are you buying it?

We are now familiar with the "empty" part of "philosophy and empty seduction." In the next two chapters, we will examine the seductions employed by the NAS which make it seem to some that empty baskets are full. In the chapter following the next two, we will show how their Platonic philosophy aids in the systematizing of their many deceptions.

CHAPTER 4

Philosophy and Empty Seduction: The Seduction, Part I

So, there's no actual evidence in the bushel baskets after all. This is the "empty" part of the apostle Paul's phrase, "philosophy and empty seduction" that describes the essential character of the reasoning systems opposed to the truth of God. Empty reasoning systems by definition have no substance, and therefore must rely upon various techniques of seduction to make them seem legitimate. The NAS writers employ many seductive techniques, of which the following are examples.

AUTHORITATIVE REPETITIVE FALSE AFFIRMATION

A major technique of seduction used by the writers of the NAS book is authoritative repetitive false affirmation. Again and again, in slightly different forms, they write that evolution is true, and that all scientists worthy to be so-called affirm that it is true. Here are some of these authoritative repetitive false affirmations, with their respective page numbers following:

. . . **the overwhelming majority of the scientific community accepts evolution as the basis for modern biology. xii.**
. . . **there is no controversy in the scientific community about whether evolution has occurred. xiii.**
. . . **evidence supporting descent with modification, as Charles Darwin termed it, is both overwhelming and compelling. xiii.**
Because of the immense body of evidence, scientists treat the occurrence of evolution as one of the most securely established of scientific facts. xiii.
. . . **our understanding of both the fact and the processes of biological evolution. 1.**

The theory of evolution is supported by so many observations and experiments that the overwhelming majority of scientists no longer question whether evolution has occurred and continues to occur . . . 3.

Is evolution a theory or a fact? It is both. 11.

. . . past and continuing occurrence of evolution is a scientific fact. 11.

Because the evidence supporting it is so strong, scientists no longer question whether biological evolution has occurred and is continuing to occur. 11.

. . . the process of biological evolution . . . [has] been overwhelmingly substantiated. 12.

. . . biological evolution has produced the diversity of living things over billions of years of Earth's history. 12.

. . . the theory of evolution is foundational scientific truth, one that has stood up to rigorous scrutiny and upon which much of human knowledge and achievement rests. 14.

Many kinds of evidence have contributed to scientific understanding of biological evolution. 17.

. . . [Scientists] are asking specific questions to learn more about how, not whether, evolution has occurred and is continuing to occur. 18.

Biological evolution is part of a compelling historical narrative that scientists have constructed over the last few centuries. 18.

. . . the appearance of life set in motion a process of biological evolution that continues to this day. 18.

Each species that lives on Earth today is the product of an evolutionary lineage . . . 24.

The occurrence of biological evolution both explains . . . diversity and accounts for its distribution. 26.

Molecular biology has confirmed and extended the conclusions about evolution drawn from other forms of science. 28.

The study of biological molecules has done more than document the evolutionary relationships among organisms. 31.

Study of all the forms of evidence discussed earlier in this booklet has led to the conclusion that humans evolved from ancestral primates. 32.

. . . today there is no scientific doubt about the close evolutionary relationships between humans and all other primates. 33.

. . . the forces responsible for the evolution of all other life forms on Earth account for the biological evolution of human characteristics. 33.

SOLVING LIGHT BOOKS

410.757.4630, Cell 410.279.5651

RBowieJ@comcast.net   www.solvinglight.com

The National Academy of Sciences (NAS) published *Science, Evolution, and Creationism* in January of this year, sending it to every school board and every science teacher in America. SOWING ATHEISM is Robert Bowie Johnson, Jr.'s timely response. What is in Mr. Johnson's book? Please see below:

"I want to put on the table, not why 85% of the members of the National Academy of Sciences reject God, I want to know why 15% of the National Academy don't . . . How come this number isn't zero?"

NAS Spokesman Neil deGrasse Tyson, p. 14

"The evo-atheists of the NAS cannot produce any actual evidence for the origin of life, for the emergence of the sexes, or for the evolution of one distinct kind of organism into another." p. 16

To conceal the lack of evidence for its evo-atheism (evolutionist-atheism), the NAS resorts to repetitive false affirmations, disguised tautologies, authoritative obfuscations, baiting and switching, and smearing apostate Christian lipstick on its atheist pig—all in order to mislead and manipulate its audience. (From a press release)

"The evo-atheists of the NAS attempt to disguise their true motives, but the very words and phrases they use in their book expose and defeat their own abominable purpose. They try to hide their atheism, but their associates betray them. They try to hide their lack of evidence, but their own language gives them away. They try to destroy creationism, but it emerges stronger than ever. They try to misrepresent Bible-believing Christians, but their scheme backfires. They try to use enchantment to overcome their lack of truth, but it winds up ensnaring them instead." p. 17

"Are your kids hungry for information on the origins and purpose of humanity? Do they wonder how they got here? Fix them another bowl of evo-atheism. That's all that's left on the shelf." p. 22

"The hierarchy of the NAS has stolen true science; they are sacrificing our children to their atheism, and at the same time, destroying our children's faith in God." p. 27

THE WASHINGTON POST FALSIFIES EVIDENCE FOR EVOLUTION, p. 31

A FALSE PROMISE, A TABOO, AND A THREAT KEEP THE EVO-ATHEISTS IN LINE, pp. 72-77

"You most likely had never heard of **Dobzhansky or Ayala** before reading this book, and yet your children must go along with their bogus philosophical presumptions or fail in science class." p. 79

"The members of the NAS hierarchy are unable to comprehend the enormous difference between *saying* something is true, and *proving* that it is true. While such a handicap has no bearing upon their respective abilities to philosophize, **it categorically disqualifies them as competent scientists.**" p. 80

BY ITS OWN DEFINITION OF RELIGIOUS BELIEF, THE NAS DEMONSTRATES THAT ITS EVO-ATHEISM IS JUST THAT—RELIGIOUS BELIEF, pp. 84-85

NATURAL SELECTION, THE KEY PRINCIPLE IN EVO-ATHEISM, TURNS OUT TO BE A MYSTICAL, MIRACULOUS, AND SUPERNATURAL FIGURE OF SPEECH. p. 86

THE EVO-ATHEISTS OF THE NAS ADMIT THE REALITY OF THEIR RELIGION. p. 88

"The hysterical rantings of the NAS propagandist Paul Henle blame the decline of science education in America on the 'unwarranted' criticism of evo-atheism. The leaders of the NAS, with their outright contempt for free speech and free thought in the science classroom, are the true villains." p. 108

Please Feel Free to Contact the Author

About 2.3 million years ago, the earliest species of *Homo*, the genus to which all modern humans belong, evolved in Africa. 34.

The sequence of fossils across Earth's sediments points unambiguously toward the occurrence of evolution. 38.

. . . evolutionary science provides one of the best examples of a deep understanding based on scientific reasoning. 39.

. . . overwhelming evidence that evolution has taken place and is continuing to occur. 39.

. . . there are no viable alternatives to evolution in the scientific literature . . . 42.

Evolution is supported by abundant evidence . . . 47.

Scientists' confidence about the occurrence of evolution is based on an overwhelming amount of supporting evidence . . . 49.

Evolution is accepted within the scientific community . . . 49.

. . . evolution itself has been so thoroughly tested that biologists are no longer examining whether evolution has occurred and is continuing to occur. 50.

. . . the fact that evolution has occurred and continues to occur. 51.

. . . no scientific controversy about the basic facts of evolution. 52.

. . . arguments that attempt to confuse students by suggesting that there are fundamental weaknesses in the science of evolution are unwarranted based on the overwhelming evidence that supports the theory. 52.

. . . [evolution] is supported by overwhelming evidence and widely accepted by the scientific community . . . 53.

Above, there are 40 of these authoritative repetitive false affirmations. In the entire NAS book, I count over 80 such false affirmations. There are only 55 pages of text in the book, and many of those pages have illustrations. It averages out to about two false affirmations per page of text. If evolution really is true, why do the NAS writers have to say so over 80 times in a 55-page book? We find the word "overwhelming" eight times within the repetitions cited above. Based on their superficial readings of the NAS book, *The Washington Post* and other gullible media have editorialized that the evidence for evolution is "overwhelming." Actual evidence for evolution is absent in the NAS book. The only thing that's

45

overwhelming is the NAS book's repetitive false assertions that the evidence is overwhelming! This isn't science—it is a form of enchantment, a work of the flesh (Galatians 5:20).

The repetitious affirmations of evolution as "truth" serve an important seductive purpose. The effect is subliminal and hypnotic: "You are getting sleepy . . . evolution is true ... evolution is proven . . . all scientists believe it . . . evolution is true . . . all scientists believe . . . when we say evolution is a theory, we mean that it's a fact . . . evolution is true . . . all scientists believe it . . .when you are finished the book, you will believe that evolution is true and all scientists believe it . . . you won't understand why these things are so, but that doesn't matter . . . evolution is true and all scientists believe it."

The beginning of Chapter 59 of Isaiah speaks of those whose "lips speak falsehood . . . and the webs of a spider are they weaving." The prey of the spider get stuck on one sticky silk strand, and, as they try to get free, they get stuck on another, and then another until they are helplessly trapped within the web. Similarly, the NAS book writers weave their web of false affirmations throughout the book. If the readers don't get stuck on page 2 or page 11 or page 18, they will begin to get stuck on page 21, and then become even more stuck on page 24, and even more stuck on page 33, and so on, until their minds are trapped within their broadly cast web of "evolution is true" affirmations. The NAS book is an atheist's hunting snare specifically designed to capture the minds of the young, the gullible, and the unstable, to get them to repeat the evo-atheist mantra as their own, and ultimately to redefine their reality, their mental framework, and their life-orientation away from God.

THE DISGUISED TAUTOLOGY DECEPTION

We've seen that a tautology is a redundancy, a statement which conveys no new or helpful information. Here's one of the many disguised tautologies from the NAS book:

. . . there is no controversy in the scientific community about whether evolution has occurred. (p. xiii).

The tautology is disguised because they infuse the term "scientific community" with a very specialized meaning. As we have seen, to the NAS "evolution is science," and those who do not accept evolution are not scientists. The scientific community, to the NAS, is made up only of those who believe in evolution. What they are saying in the above sentence is that "there is no controversy among those scientists who accept that evolution has occurred about whether evolution has occurred." Their sentence thus has no meaning, merit or relevance whatsoever in the evolution-creation debate. It's a dog chasing its own tail. Their intent is to downplay and disguise the fact that there *is a huge* controversy. That's why they published their book, to respond to the controversy! But now if they are to be believed, there isn't one! The only thing their disguised tautology proves is that the NAS book writers have the ability to manipulate language in their favor in order to give a false impression of what the facts are. Here are some more examples from their book:

. . . there are no viable alternatives to evolution in the scientific [evolution-promoting] literature . . . (p. 42).
(or put another way, "No alternatives to evolution exist in the evolution-promoting literature").

Evolution is accepted within the scientific [evolution-promoting] community . . . (p. 49).

In both sentences, they say basically the same thing twice—that's what makes them tautologies. There is no information in the predicate not already inherent in the subject. The NAS writers use tautologies such as these over and over to persuade the readers that evolution is true. Besides being deceptive, their statements convey no useful information regardless of their length or complexity. We already know that evolutionists believe in evolution!

One of the great things about tautologies, from the NAS standpoint, is that they cannot be proven false. "Evolution is accepted within the evolution-promoting community." How true! "There are no viable alternatives to evolution in the evolution-promoting literature." You got that right, sister! This technique also is a form of enchantment.

AUTHORITATIVE OBFUSCATION

In 2002, Illustra Media produced a fascinating DVD/VHS called *Unlocking the Mystery of Life: The Scientific Case for Intelligent Design*. If you haven't seen it, I recommend it highly to you. From its own description:

Using state-of-the-art computer animation, "Unlocking the Mystery of Life" transports you into the interior of the living cell to explore systems and machines that bear the unmistakable hallmarks of design. Discover the intricacy of a microscopic bacterial rotary motor, which spins at 100,000 rpm. Within the nucleus explore the wonder of DNA, a thread-like molecule that stores instructions to build the essential components of every living organism. It is part of a biological information processing system more complex and more powerful than any computer network. This compelling documentary examines an idea with the power to revolutionize our understanding of life . . . and to unlock the mystery of its origin.

The video is an outgrowth of the work of Michael J. Behe of Lehigh University who wrote *Darwin's Black Box: The Biochemical Challenge to Evolution*, and who coined the term "irreducible complexity." As a household example of irreducible complexity, Behe chooses the mousetrap—a machine that could not function if any of its pieces were missing, and whose pieces have no value except as parts of the whole. What is true of the mousetrap, he says, is even truer of the bacterial flagellum, a whip-like cellular organelle used for propulsion that operates like an outboard motor. That microscopic motor includes a water-cooled rotary engine, forward and reverse gears, a direction-reversing capability within one-quarter of a turn, a hard-wired signal transduction system with short-term memory, a proton motive-force drive system, and self-assembly and repair.

The possibility that this intricate array could have arisen through evolutionary modification is virtually nil, Behe argues, and that points to intelligent design.

The NAS book, however, asserts that irreducible complexity is "disproven by the findings of modern biology," and presents its "proof" in the following paragraph:

> . . . [T]here is no single, uniform structure that is found in all flagellar bacteria. There are many types of flagella, some simpler than others, and many species of bacteria do not have flagella to aid in their movement. Thus, other components of bacterial cell membranes are likely the precursors of the proteins found in various flagella. In addition, some bacteria inject toxins into other cells through proteins that are secreted from the bacterium and that are very similar in their molecular structure to the proteins in parts of the flagella. This similarity indicates a common evolutionary origin, where small changes in the structure and organization of the secretory proteins could serve as the basis for flagellar proteins. Thus, flagellar proteins are not irreducibly complex. (p. 41).

Do you notice the utter lack of clarity here? The reason for their lack of clarity is that their own minds are not clear as to what they are saying. Just on the basis of the logic of language, their refutation of irreducible complexity fails. They draw a factual conclusion from a perplexingly derived (to say the least) possibility. In the next to last sentence they write that "secretory proteins *could serve* as the basis for flagellar proteins" (my emphasis). All they can logically infer as their conclusion is, "Thus, flagellar proteins *may not be* irreducibly complex." But as is most typical, they leap from speculation to "fact" without comment.

Average readers accept the NAS's "authoritative obfuscation" because, even though their "refutation" of intelligent design is obscure, complicated, and confusing, they figure that the NAS authorities must know what they are talking about.

BAIT AND SWITCH

The NAS writers present an example of non-controversial changes within a species (microevolution, sometimes called horizontal evolution), and then switch to writing about the extremely controversial molecules-to-man evolution, falsely implying that the evidence for one adds credence to the other. It is somewhat ironic that their bait in this "bait and switch" ruse is a small fish that lives in the Aripo River on the island of Trinidad. They write:

Guppies that live in the river are eaten by a larger species of fish that eats both juveniles and adults, while guppies that live in the small streams feeding into the river are eaten by a smaller fish that preys primarily on small juveniles. The guppies in the river mature faster, are smaller, and give birth to more and smaller offspring than the guppies in the streams do because guppies with these traits are better able to avoid their predator in the river than are larger guppies. When guppies were taken from the river and introduced into a stream without a preexisting population of guppies, they evolved traits like those of the stream guppies within about 20 generations. (p. 7).

These relocated guppies did not "evolve" traits in their new environment, rather they manifested them. As Henry M. Morris has pointed out, "[M]any varieties [are] capable of arising within each kind, in order to enable each basic kind to cope with changing environments without becoming extinct."[1] This is an ability the different species owe to their Creator.

After setting the bait, the NAS writers immediately switch to molecules-to-man evolution (so-called and unproven macroevolution, sometimes referred to as vertical evolution) and present the following utterly unfounded inference from the story of the guppies: "Incremental evolutionary changes can, over what are usually very long periods of time, give rise to new types of organisms, including new species."

Thus, the NAS writers trick the casual reader into thinking that they have just been presented with evidence for molecules-to-man evolution, when they have not.

SLAPPING SCIENCE LIPSTICK ON THE NO-EVIDENCE PIG

"Slapping lipstick on the pig" refers to deceptive efforts used to cosmetically hide or camouflage something ugly, or better yet, to make it seem like there's nothing ugly there at all. Out of millions of species on this planet, the evo-atheists cannot specifically trace back the "evolutionary" ancestry of one of them even a single "evolutionary" generation. That's an ugly embarrassment and an ugly fact. The NAS writers have to slap some lipstick on their "no-evidence" pig.

Throughout their book, the NAS writers use the word "science" 402 times, the word "scientific" 116 times, and the word "scientists" 66 times for a total of 584 times. For the evo-atheists, those words are the best lipstick money can buy. They point out in the very first sentence of their book that, "Scientific and technological advances have had profound effects on human life." They mention, among other things, the computers, cars, airplanes, and medicines we use to fend off and cure diseases. Who isn't grateful to "science" and "scientific" research and to "scientists" for these things?

The NAS book writers smear their "sciency" lipstick all over their evidence-shy pig. With only 55 pages of text in the book, the word "science" and its derivatives appear on average more than 10 times per page. That's a lot of lipstick, but they need every bit of it to hide the ugly fact that they do not have any evidence.

Let's change that metaphor a bit. All of those "science" words are a lot of cheese sauce to put on undercooked broccoli, and they are a lot of icing to put on a salty cake. The NAS hierarchy is fortunate that most of their naïve readers, including influential publishers, editors, newsmen, and television producers, are content just to nibble on the cheese sauce, and snack on the icing. Let's go back to the original lipstick metaphor: these media big shots have been tricked into making out with the National Academy of Sciences' no-evidence pig.

SLAPPING CHRISTIAN LIPSTICK ON THE ATHEIST HOG

The NAS hierarchy knows how ugly their atheism looks to the God-fearing citizens of America, so they've got to smear a lot of lipstick on their atheist hog. They use liberal, apostate Christianity for that purpose without, of course, using the words "liberal" or "apostate." The NAS book asserts:

As *Science, Evolution, and Creationism* makes clear, the evidence for evolution can be fully compatible with religious faith . . . Many religious denominations and individual religious leaders have issued statements acknowledging the occurrence of evolution and pointing out that evolution and faith do not conflict. (pp. xiii, 13).

By "religious denominations" they mean mostly those of liberal, mainstream Christianity. The theme of the "compatibility" of evolution and Christianity appears throughout their book. They smear the lipstick of liberal, apostate Christianity all over their ugly atheist hog. By the time they complete their deception, you'd think the atheist NAS book authors did their writing in church pews. This particular seduction of theirs is so wicked, contemptible and devious that we need to devote the entire next chapter to it.

CHAPTER 5

Philosophy and Empty Seduction: The Seduction, Part II

In this chapter, we go into detail about how the NAS writers smear the lipstick of liberal, apostate Christendom all over their atheist hog, seducing millions of church-goers in the process. The seduction works like this:

Evolution comes to the door of a Christian church. Knock! Knock! The pastor answers the door.

EVOLUTION: Hello, Pastor. I'm Evolution. May I come in?

PASTOR: I don't think so. You kind of frighten me.

EVOLUTION: No need to be frightened, Pastor. Science approves of me.

PASTOR: Well, in that case, you can come in. But wait, Atheism isn't with you, is he?

EVOLUTION: Oh no, Pastor, I wouldn't associate with Atheism.

PASTOR: Fine, then. Come on in. We're happy to have you. I'm teaching today on the serpent as a symbol of evil, and of Satan, the Adversary.

EVOLUTION: I'm sorry, Pastor, but that won't do. We're all descended from serpents through chance and natural selection. No one life form is any more special than any other. Blaming the serpent is not politically correct.

PASTOR: Are you sure Atheism didn't sneak in here with you?

EVOLUTION: Oh no, Pastor. Atheism is nowhere around here. I wouldn't lie to you.

PASTOR: Well then, I'm going to teach on the truth of Noah
             with his ark saving humanity through the Flood.

EVOLUTION: No, Pastor, you can't do that. I'd be a mess if there
             had been such a Flood. It didn't happen. Stories
             like that are all metaphors. They mean anything
             you want them to mean. Trust your own mind.
             That's how you tell what's true and what's false.

PASTOR: You know, Evolution, you said Atheism isn't with
             you, but you haven't said how God fits into your
             ideas.

EVOLUTION: Who?

Does that sound far-fetched to you? It shouldn't. On a full page, the NAS book draws special attention to a letter signed by more than 10,000 "Christian" clergy members who have welcomed molecules-to-man evolution into their churches. The headline at the top of the page reads: "Excerpts of Statements by Religious Leaders Who See No Conflict Between Their Faith and Science." By "Science," of course, they mean evo-atheism.

The obvious problem here is that it is simply not possible to be a Christian in any meaningful sense of the word, and at the same time, embrace the tenets of atheistic evolution. On His Father's side, the Scriptures refer to Jesus Christ as the "Son of God." On His mother's side, the Scriptures refer to Him as the "Son of Man," not as the son of reptiles. Christ maintained that the Word of God is truth. Evo-atheism contradicts the Word of God. How can one have any kind of faith in a Christ who lies about the inspiration of the Scriptures by God, and lies about his descent from Adam through Noah?

And yet, as of this writing, 1,500 more "Christian" clergy members have signed this letter that is the centerpiece of The Clergy Letter Project.

Michael Zimmerman, Dean of the College of Liberal Arts and Sciences at Butler University, is the brains behind the project. It began in the fall of 2004 when Zimmerman worked with clergy in Wisconsin to prepare and present a statement supporting evolution to the school board in Grantsburg that was considering the authorized mention of creationism in science classes. According to Zimmerman:

The response was overwhelming. In a few weeks, nearly 200 clergy signed the statement, which we sent to the Grantsburg school board on December 16, 2004. Additionally, groups of educators and scientists sent letters to the Grantsburg School Board and to the Superintendent of Schools protesting these [creationist] policies. In response to all of this attention, as well as the efforts of others, the Grantsburg School Board retracted their policies. The outpouring of support from clergy around the country encouraged me to make this a nationwide project . . . By doing so, we are educating thousands and elevating the world-wide discussion of this important topic.

Zimmerman's avowed effort is to clear up "one of the most basic misconceptions about evolution . . . that it conflicts with Christianity and thus Christians have to choose between their religion and modern science." No misconception needs to be cleared up. "Modern science," Zimmerman's euphemism for evo-atheism, conflicts with Christianity at the most basic level. And yet, thousands of gullible "Christian" pastors have quickly jumped on the bandwagon and signed the letter. Zimmerman describes them as "fully comfortable with their faith and evolution." These pastors ignore these specific warnings from the apostle Paul:

Yet from profane prattling stand aloof, for they [the prattlers] will be progressing to more irreverence, and their word will spread like gangrene . . . (II Timothy 2:16).

O Timothy, that which is committed to you, guard, turning aside from the profane prattling and antipathies of falsely named "knowledge," which some are professing. As to the faith they swerve (I Timothy 6:20-21).

The Greek word translated "prattling" in the above passages is *keno-phonia*, empty-sound. Remember the empty bushel baskets from Chapter 3? In this case, the "profane prattling" is the sound of the evo-atheists, tirelessly insisting that they have evidence, echoing back from the empty baskets.

According to the Scriptures, who are these thousands of apostate pastors who have opened the doors of their "Christian" churches to Darwinian evolution and atheism? In II Thessalonians 2:3, the apostle Paul refers to them as part of a genuine "apostasy" and predicts its coming to fruition. Apostasy comes from the Greek word *apo-stasis* meaning from-standing. Nominal Christians stand away from the teaching of the Scriptures as the Word of God, and bring in contradictory man-made beliefs to which they give the dominant credence.

Paul described some specifics of the apostasy in these passages:

Now the spirit is saying explicitly, that in subsequent eras some will be withdrawing from the faith, giving heed to deceiving spirits and the teachings of demons, in the hypocrisy of false expressions, their own conscience having been cauterized . . . (I Timothy 4:1-2).

For the era will be when they will not tolerate sound teaching, but their hearing being tickled, they will heap up for themselves teachers in accord with their own desires, and, indeed, they will be turning their hearing away from the truth, yet will be turned aside to myths (II Timothy 4:3-4).

We saw in Chapter 3 that there is no real evidence for molecules-to-man evolution. This makes it a myth, just as Paul writes.

In his epistles, Paul refers to Adam, Eve, and Noah as historical ancestors of mankind. Paul also refers to the transgression by the first couple in Eden and to Noah's Flood as historical events. Molecules-to-man evolution denies that humanity originated in Eden with Adam and Eve, and it denies Noah and the world-wide Flood which Moses, Jesus, and Peter, in addition to Paul, assert actually occurred. The evo-atheists of the NAS, and now more than 11,500 "Christian" pastors believe that all of humanity is descended by chance from reptiles, and beyond that, from a single-celled randomite (we can't call it a creature because that implies creation) which emerged by chemical chance from some kind

56

of "primordial soup" two billion years ago. The two teachings are utterly incompatible.

The differences go way beyond origins. Evo-atheists and apostate Christians (also now evo-atheists) do not look to Paul or Christ for the truth but to Darwin and "science." It is a simple question of authority. They stand away from God and His Word, and toward men—Darwin and the hierarchy of the NAS. They abandon trust in the Creator and His Son for trust in men. We read in Proverbs 30:5-6:

Every word of God is pure: he is a shield unto them that put their trust in Him.

Add thou not unto his words, lest he reprove thee, and thou be found a liar.

These thousands of apostate pastors add the words of Darwin and the NAS to their idea of what they hypocritically refer to in their Clergy Letter as "Holy Scripture" and thus identify themselves as liars.

These thousands of apostate pastors deny II Timothy 3:16: "All scripture is inspired by God, and is beneficial for teaching . . ." Just what, then, is Christian about their ministries?

During his earthly ministry to Israel, Jesus often experienced the attacks of religious leaders who claimed their man-centered authority trumped His. According to the Scriptures, Jesus is the Son of God in Whom "all the treasures of wisdom and knowledge are concealed" (Colossians 2:3). Jesus confronted the Pharisees who challenged His authority, calling them blind and stupid (Matthew 23 and elsewhere). I am part of the body of Christ and I believe in the authority of the Scriptures. So the NAS, by trotting out statements from apostate Christians in their defense, is basically saying to me and all others who share my views, "Look at all the spiritually blind and stupid people we have on our side!"

The Greek word translated as stupid is *moron*, where we get our word for a mentally dull and sluggish person. In my judgment, only morons—more than 11,500 morons in this case—could sign a letter maintaining that the "timeless truths of the Bible" are compatible with

57

the billions of unpredictable aberrations of evo-atheism. What do these apostate morons celebrate at their Sunday services, the lies about humanity's origins told by Moses, Jesus, and Paul?

Jesus also referred to the Pharisees who challenged His authority as "Serpents! Progeny of vipers!" (Matthew 23:33). Isn't it revealing that today's "Christian" apostates welcome the idea that they themselves, and their flocks, are the progeny of reptiles?

Paul urged believers to follow him as he followed Christ. As we shall see, the Clergy Letter urges "Christians" to follow Michael Zimmerman as he follows the religious doctrines of the evo-atheist hierarchy of the National Academy of Sciences.

Zimmerman claims that he did not write the letter himself, but rather commissioned a minister from the United Church of Christ to write it. I asked Zimmerman to please identify this letter-writer so I could contact him with my many questions. Zimmerman refused. I also asked the professor to reveal his own religious persuasion. Again, he refused, writing, "I'm unwilling to discuss my own religious affiliation because it is absolutely irrelevant to the work of the Clergy Letter Project." So, we have a letter signed by 11,500 "Christian" clergy, commissioned by a man who refuses to reveal his religious affiliation, and written by a man whom we are unable to identify.

In responding to the authors of the Clergy Letter sentence by sentence, below, we'll gain more insight into the muddled thinking patterns of the evo-atheists and their liberal, apostate "Christian" buddies. Sentences from the Clergy Letter appear in italics.

Within the community of Christian believers there are areas of dispute and disagreement, including the proper way to interpret Holy Scripture.

Men's biases have gotten in the way of letting the Scriptures speak for themselves since they were first written. Mistranslation causes big problems. The disputes and disagreements concern differences in men's teachings, not contradictions in the Word of God itself. The risen Christ called and saved the apostle Paul on the road to Damascus, taught him, and appointed him "a teacher of the nations in knowledge and truth" (I Timothy 2:7). Paul explained to Timothy how to be sure the true teaching remained intact:

And what things you hear from me through many witnesses, these commit to *faithful* men, who shall be *competent* to teach others also (II Timothy 2:2, my emphases).

That's all you have to do: teach what Paul taught, and follow him as he follows Christ. You may run into some things that require more time for study, but overall, if you stick to Paul, your teaching will be fundamentally truthful and accurate. The problem is that you don't have any idea what Paul taught, and this isn't the place to explain his teachings to you in any detail. One thing Paul did not teach, however, was that mankind evolved out of slime by mindless chemistry and then through rodents and reptiles as a result of millions of genetic copying errors, or unpredictable aberrations.

Neither one of you is in the least way competent to teach anyone about the true teaching for Christians today. And yet, your entire letter is a presumption on your part that you are indeed competent to explain "the proper way to interpret Holy Scripture," all the while ignoring the teachings of the apostle appointed by Jesus Christ Himself for that purpose. You're off to a bad start.

While virtually all Christians take the Bible seriously and hold it to be authoritative in matters of faith and practice, the overwhelming majority do not read the Bible literally, as they would a science textbook.

Tens of millions of Christians read the Bible literally; that is, as the truth—whether expressed as matters of fact or in figures of speech. A Gallup poll of the American people, taken before you published your letter, revealed that 45% of the American people are creationists. When pollsters asked whether humans were created in a form much as they are today, within the last ten thousand years, they said yes. Mr. X, you didn't do any research and instead expressed a vague feeling of yours as a fact. You made up a fact to support your apostate point of view. Your "overwhelming majority" is more than a gross exaggeration; it is flat wrong. By "overwhelming majority" you mean the overwhelming majority of your pals inside your liberal, apostate bubble.

We can see by looking at your language in this sentence that you express an obvious contradiction. How is it possible to take the Bible seriously and authoritatively, yet not take it literally; that is, as truth?

Because a few people, or a great many people claiming to be Christians do not read the Bible literally in no way indicates that it is not *meant* to be taken literally, as absolute truth. That determination must be made on the basis of what the Scriptures say about themselves, and they say over and over again that they are the Spirit-breathed words of the Creator, and they are not to be adulterated.

Where do you get the idea that science textbooks can be taken literally, as truth? The key operative principle of molecules-to-man evolution, natural selection, is itself an un-literal figure of speech. I don't have a science textbook in front of me, but I do have the NAS book from which the textbooks take their cue, and it consistently uses the decidedly un-literal subjunctive mood.

Tiktaalik [a fish fossil from which we are allegedly descended] *may have lived* somewhat before or somewhat after the ancestral species that gave rise to all of today's limbed animals, including humans. The evolutionary lineage that contained Tiktaalik *may have gone extinct*, as shown in this diagram by the short line branching from the main evolutionary lineage, or it *may have been part* of the evolutionary line leading to all modern tetrapods (animals with four legs) (my emphases).

Is that what you two call literal language? You don't find such iffy language in the Scriptures. Also, look up on the Web "Ernst Haeckel's Fake Drawings" and the "Peppered Moth Hoax." These still appear in many science textbooks, as does that fanciful drawing of a fish crawling out of the water and turning into a man. These things are not literal; they're not figurative either: they're just phony. Just for fun, Google "evolution hoaxes" and see what else you find.

I know, Zimmerman, as a result of our email correspondence that you and Mister X think most of what is written in the Scriptures is metaphorical. As you wrote: ". . . the power of metaphor in the Bible is so much more important than the 'facts' that are included." Whom were you quoting, Paul or Jesus?

I think I can say without fear of contradiction that the Bible contains more figures of speech than any other book. These include metaphors, similes, parables, implications, allegories, visions, signs, shadows, metonymies, synecdoche, condescensions, hyperboles, ironies, and personifications.

When the Lord God says, "The heavens are My throne, And the earth is My footstool" (Isaiah 66:1), we know that it is not literal. But yet the magnificence of God represented in this combination metaphor (likeness), association (the throne is associated with rule), and condescension (ascribing what is human to the Deity), is not false. When Jesus told his disciples that He was about to wake Lazarus out of sleep, they initially took it literally, but it wasn't meant that way. This figure of speech, not true as to fact, foreshadowed the great truth that the death of Lazarus was like taking a nap, and that Christ would soon rouse him from it. Discerning Christians understand the difference between figurative and literal language.

Most scriptural passages are unequivocally literal. When, in praying to His Father, Jesus says, "Thy Word is truth" (John 17:17), it is meant quite literally. So are the passages pertaining to the original creation, the making of Adam "of soil from the ground," and Noah's making of the ark from sulphur wood.

Unbelievers such as the two of you typically dismiss the Scriptures as all metaphorical, so that no "facts" remain for you to consider.

By the way, do you both enjoy helping the NAS smear the lipstick of liberal, apostate Christendom all over their atheist hog? It is your atheist hog, too, isn't it? Even with all the lipstick you're haphazardly slapping on it, the atheist hog is still just as repulsive as ever.

Many of the beloved stories found in the Bible—the Creation, Adam and Eve, Noah and the ark—convey timeless truths about God, human beings, and the proper relationship between Creator and creation expressed in the only form capable of transmitting these truths from generation to generation.

How are you able to embrace the Darwinian notion that you are basically pond scum rearranged over countless eons by chance, and yet find the Genesis creation account to be "beloved," or dear to your hearts? You don't believe the account of the serpent deluding Eve in the Garden of Eden, bringing death to all humanity, and you don't believe the account of all mankind, save eight souls, drowning violently in a world-wide deluge, yet you dearly love both of these "stories." Why? What's to love?

We're not talking about Aesop's Fables or Mother Goose rhymes here. The Word of God claims to be "living and operative, and keen above any two-edged sword, and penetrating up to the parting of soul and spirit, both of the articulations and marrow, and is a judge of the sentiments and thoughts of the heart" (Hebrews 4:12). Zimmerman, your first name, Michael, is derived from that of God's messenger to Daniel during the Babylonian captivity. This book is published in 2008 because it has been 2008 years since Christ's birth. Your cavalier dismissal of the truth of the Scriptures is unwise and unscholarly.

If you were students in my class, I'd assign you this task for homework: List fifty of the "timeless truths about God" found in the Bible, to which you refer. Would these be among them?

All good giving and every perfect gratuity is from above, descending from the Father of lights, in Whom there is no mutation or shadow from revolving motion (James 1:17).

Now no one can be slaving for two lords, for either he will be hating the one and loving the other, or will be upholding one and despising the other. You cannot be slaving for God and mammon (Matthew 6:24).

No, the above verses would not appear on your list, neither would any other Scriptures for that matter. I'd be especially interested in your specific "timeless truths" about "the proper relationship between Creator and creation," because a few sentences later you assert that what man thinks trumps what God says. Your love for the "timeless truths about God" revealed in the Bible is a condescending sham.

Religious truth is of a different order from scientific truth. Its purpose is not to convey scientific information but to transform hearts.

The same God Who created nature also inspired the Sacred Scriptures. There is no contradiction between the Scriptures (in the original languages) and nature. When in Genesis 1:11, God says: "Verdant shall become the land with verdure; and with herbage seeding seed for its from-kind and for its likeness, and with the fruit tree whose seed is in it yielding fruit for its from-kind, on the land," we are learning about the generation of plants and trees. When we read in Job 26:7 that God "stretched out the north over the chaos, hanging the earth upon nothingness," we are learning something about the solar system and gravity.

When Jesus tells us, "God is Spirit" (John 4:24), and then Paul writes that all is out of Him (Romans 11:36), we are learning about the very foundation of matter itself. When we read in Genesis 1:31 that God is creating "great monsters," we are learning about the existence of dinosaurs before Noah's Flood. When God refers to Himself in Isaiah 40:22 as "sitting over the circle of the earth," we are learning about the shape of our planet. When we read in Genesis 7:11 that, pertaining to the beginning of Noah's Flood, "rent are all the springs of the vast submerged chaos," we are getting a geology lesson. When Paul tells us that Christ now is "making His home in light inaccessible" (I Timothy 6:16), we realize how limited our perceptions are, and how feeble our abilities to measure all that lies beyond the senses.

And please don't try to portray the Scriptures as merely appealing to the emotions with the "transform hearts" bit, since you both fall into the category of those who have become vain in their reasonings, and whose unintelligent hearts have been darkened (Romans 1:21). Is "the peace of Christ arbitrating in your hearts," (Colossians 3:15) or is it the dogma of evo-atheism? And speaking of the heart as a moral center, why should a person descended by chance from reptiles and worms be subject to any moral restraints?

We the undersigned, Christian clergy from many different traditions, believe that the timeless truths of the Bible and the discoveries of modern science may comfortably coexist.

By the "discoveries of modern science" you mean the claims the evo-atheists make about humanity's origins. That's what this Clergy Letter is all about, not improvements in laser surgery. Again, your avowal is that the supposed evolution of mankind over millions of years through reptiles, rodents, dogs, and apes is compatible with certain, yet again unspecified, "timeless truths of the Bible."

That God created Adam in an ancient paradise and "breathed into him the breath of the living" can't be one of those truths. That Noah, a descendant of Adam, brought himself, seven other humans, and hundreds of pairs of animals through a world-wide flood lasting nearly a year can't be one of those truths. That Jesus Christ was descended on his mother's side from Adam through Noah can't be one of those truths. Darwinism insists that Christ's mother, Mary, and Christ Himself on His mother's side, did not come through Noah and Adam but rather, through rodents and reptiles. I ask you again, what "timeless truths of the Bible" are you referring to?

Your choice of the word "coexist" is interesting, because this is basically true, except for the "comfortably" part. The Word of God and evo-atheism do coexist, but only in the sense that light and darkness coexist. They are opposite and incompatible, but they do coexist. Darkness is the absence of light. Light, figuratively, is that which enables spiritual sight. You reject Paul's teachings, and, thus, that he was commissioned by Christ to open the eyes of the nations, and "to turn them about from darkness to light" (Acts 26:18), preferring instead the unfruitful works of evo-atheistic darkness.

64

You two, however, have convinced thousands of pastors, and in turn, many members of their flocks, that human evolution from reptiles is light. Jesus said, "If, then, the light that is in you is darkness, how dense is the darkness!" (Matthew 6:23). May God grant you repentance to sober up out of the trap of the Adversary.

We believe that the theory of evolution is a foundational scientific truth, one that has stood up to rigorous scrutiny and upon which much of human knowledge and achievement rests.

We've seen that the evolution of all life from a single cell from two billion years ago allegedly consists of genetic copying mistakes operated upon in some undefined way by the figure of speech known as natural selection. In Chapter 3, we saw that there is no evidence for this. There is nothing rigorous at all about speculation, and that's what it is. And Mr. X, your many factual, logical, and contextual errors show that your own letter does not stand up to slapdash scrutiny, much less "rigorous scrutiny." You are obviously not a "rigorous scrutiny" kind of guy, so how would you know what standards of fact and accuracy molecules-to-man evolution meets or does not meet? Who told you evolution stands up to rigorous scrutiny? Zimmerman?

Darwin and his theory of evolution do nothing but obscure knowledge and take false credit for achievements in real science. Complete this sentence: If it weren't for Darwin's theory of molecules-to-man evolution, mankind wouldn't . . .

To reject this truth or to treat it as "one theory among others" is to deliberately embrace scientific ignorance and transmit such ignorance to our children.

You exalt evolution above all. Has believing in it become the new greatest commandment, displacing the foremost precept as expressed by Christ in Mark 12:30?

You shall be loving the Lord your God out of your whole heart and out of your whole soul, and out of your whole comprehension, and out of your whole strength. This is the foremost precept.

You can offer no evidence for your premise that evolution is valid and true, so you try to bring into disrepute the character of those who disagree. According to the two of you (an atheist and an apostate), by believing and upholding the Word of God, I and many others are "deliberately" transmitting ignorance to our children. Once again, you have it backwards. What kind of monster parents teach their children that they're descended from rodents and reptiles?

We believe that among God's good gifts are human minds capable of critical thought and that the failure to fully employ this gift is a rejection of the will of our Creator.

Let's make a bet. I'll give you a million dollars for every passage of Scripture you find that states or infers that God desires that we exalt our flesh-minds and/or our wisdom over Him and His Word. You give me just $100 every time I produce a passage from Scripture that says the wisdom of God is supreme to the thinking and "wisdom" of men. Which of us do you think will have a million dollars first?

I draw your attention to this Scripture:

. . . the disposition of the flesh is enmity to God, for it is not subject to the law of God, for neither is it able. Now those who are in flesh are not able to please God (Romans 8:7-8).

Your Clergy Letter reads as if this may be found in the Bible:

Thus saith the Lord, "I give unto thee critical thought, so that ye may criticize my word, and ye may usurp the authority of the apostle Paul, but yeah and verily, thou shalt not criticize evolution for it is the ultimate theory-fact, and not merely one among many."

The Scriptures admonish us over and over to have *no* confidence in the flesh. You and your apostate letter-signers urge putting *all* confidence in the flesh. Again, you have it just backwards. Feasting upon human reason leads away from truth, not toward it.

If you accept molecules-to-man evolution, you've got to believe you came into being by chance. What's "the will of our Creator" doing as a phrase in your letter? Where did He come from?

To argue that God's loving plan of salvation for humanity precludes the full employment of the God-given faculty of reason is to attempt to limit God, an act of hubris.

I'm self-taught in the ancient literature field, so it surprises me that with your liberal academic background, Zimmerman, you don't understand what hubris is, because it originated as an ancient Greek concept. Hubris is self-pride and overbearing arrogance, an abject lack of humility. Proverbs 16:18 sums up the ancient and modern understanding of hubris: "Pride goeth before destruction, and a haughty spirit before a fall." You have it just backwards again. You are maintaining that hubris is the *failure to exalt oneself* and the reasonings of one's mind over God.

Hubris was considered the greatest sin in the ancient Greek world. Achilles' treatment of Hector's corpse, dragging it around the walls of Troy, is a classic example of it. The words of the Bible claim to be "Spirit and Life." By denying the Bible's inspiration, you kill it, and like Achilles, you drag its deadened content before men, pumping your fists and proclaiming from your chariot of reason the superiority of the mind of man over the Word of God.

To reason means to lay facts in relation to one another so as to be the basis of opinion. The Word of God claims to be absolute truth, and in no way mere opinion. What you are saying about our faculty of reason is the opposite of what of what the Scriptures say about it:

All be doing without murmurings and reasonings, that you may become blameless and artless, children of God, flawless, in the midst of a generation crooked and perverse . . . (Philippians 2:14).

I am intending, then, that men pray in every place, lifting up benign hands, apart from anger and reasoning (I Timothy 2:8).

You mention "God's loving plan of salvation." Do you even know what that is? Paul expresses how we are to approach others with God's salvation message:

For Christ, then, are we ambassadors, as of God entreating through us. We are beseeching for Christ's sake, "Be conciliated to God!" For the One not knowing sin, He makes to be a sin offering for our sakes that we may be becoming God's righteousness in Him (II Corinthians 5:20-21).

You two, and all the signers of your letter, are ambassadors for Darwin and evo-science. The Scriptures speak of mankind's conciliation to God through Christ. Mr. X, you preach conciliation to the evo-atheists at the National Academy of Sciences through Zimmerman. Also, Mr. X, you know that God commissioned Christ (John 11:42), and that in turn, Christ commissioned Paul (Acts 26:17). Zimmerman commissioned you, but who commissioned Zimmerman? Who is entreating through him, and for what purpose?

We urge school board members to preserve the integrity of the science curriculum by affirming the teaching of the theory of evolution as a core component of human knowledge.

That part of the "science curriculum" concerning molecules-to-man evolution is nothing more than empty seduction. There is no "integrity" (veracity, reliability, or uprightness) in duping school boards, educators, teachers, and students. Evolution is arrant speculation, not knowledge. It is not the "core component" of anything real.

We ask that science remain science and that religion remain religion, two very different, but complementary, forms of truth.

I have no clue as to what you are trying to get across here, in this last sentence of your letter. Throughout, you've been trying to make the case that Christian churches ought to *welcome* molecules-to-man evolution as part of their beliefs. Now you want them to remain separate somehow?

Why don't you quote some Scripture in your letter? I know why: there's not a single verse you can cite that backs up your position. You'd think that a letter about doctrine written by a "Christian" clergyman would mention Jesus at least once.

The evo-atheists at the NAS really appreciate you guys. They even invited all the Clergy Project Letter people in the Washington, D. C. area to their January party announcing the publication of their new book. Your contribution to the evo-atheist NAS hierarchy is two-fold: you help them keep the valid God hypothesis out of the science classroom, while at the same time helping them introduce the poison of their atheism into America's churches. I can't give you the total credit for seducing all of the signers of your letter, however, because most of them had to come to you willing to be seduced. Still, all you've really done is spread *a whole lot* of liberal, apostate Christian lipstick on an ugly atheist hog. You haven't succeeded in covering up the atheist hog: you've just smeared lies all over it.

I thought at first that the phenomena I was observing here—11,500 ministers holding two conflicting spiritual ideas in their minds at the same time—was something akin to cognitive dissonance. But as I looked deeper into it, I learned cognitive dissonance carries with it an uncomfortable tension, which is completely absent here. It must be cognitive obliviousness, then. These pastors cannot possibly understand the moral and spiritual implications of signing your letter, can they? Darwin seated with Christ on His throne is too blasphemous a picture to contemplate.

Let me close my response to your letter, and this chapter, by speaking directly to the pastors who have signed your letter.

How many of you pastors who have signed the Clergy Letter can say "Jesus is Lord"? If you can say that, why do you allow Zimmerman, on behalf of the evo-atheists at the National Academy of Sciences, to usurp His authority? I don't feel sorry for you, but I do feel sorry for the children in your congregations who are being fed a steady diet of lies and confusion, and who are not being taught the difference between good and evil. If you can't say "Jesus is Lord," do the right thing and change the name of your church. Take any mention of Christ out of it, and henceforth do not refer to yourselves as Christians. The children deserve that much.

CHAPTER 6

Philosophy and Empty Seduction: The Philosophy

Science, Evolution, and Creationism is not about evidence, but rather about a philosophy of science, a limited pattern of thinking with roots in the ancient philosophy of Plato.

Who, specifically, is responsible for the NAS book? Eighteen committee members, under the direction of a committee chairman were charged with producing it, all credentialed academics. Where did academia itself originate? It began in ancient Athens, in about 387 BC, with the Academy of Plato. All of Plato's Dialogues survive, and are taught throughout our colleges and universities.

An overlooked warning about Platonic philosophy appears in the Scriptures. In Matthew 7:13, Jesus said, "Enter through the cramped gate, for *broad* is the gate and spacious is the way which is leading away into destruction, and many are those entering through it" (my emphasis). The word "broad" in Greek is *platu* or *plato*. Plato's real name was Aristokles which means "the glory of the best." People called him Plato because of his broad shoulders or because of his broad forehead. "Plato is the gate . . . leading away into destruction . . ."

Plato's mouthpiece was Sokrates. Plato's Academy, and of course Sokrates himself, excluded the idea of a Creator, as do their "intellectual" spawn, modern academia. For Plato and Sokrates, it is all about the exaltation of the human mind above all. In Plato's Dialogue, *Crito*, Sokrates affirms that he must be guided by reason only (46b). The Greek word for mind is *nous*. In Plato's Dialogue, *Cratylus*, Sokrates refers to "The nous, the mind . . . the pure nous" as "the divine in us" (396b). In Plato's Dialogue, *Philebus*, Sokrates said, ". . . since all philosophers assert with one voice that mind is the king of heaven and earth—in reality they are magnifying themselves. And perhaps they are right" (28c). Remember Zimmerman and Mr. X, in the last chapter, exalting the mind as the ultimate arbiter of all, above even the pronouncements of God in the Scriptures? They are simply harmonizing their own man-centered philosophies with the ancient Sokratic chorus.

Some people think of Platonic philosophy as an objective search for truth. It is no such thing. It involves presenting one's soul to be charmed by the reigning philosophical authority. Sokrates' adoring student, Charmides, says to his master, "I am certain that I greatly need the charm (Greek = *epode*) and nothing on my part will stand in the way of my being charmed by you every day until you say that it is enough" (*Charmides*, 176b). In order to become part of the great intellectual elite, Charmides offers himself "to be enchanted" by the words and authority of Sokrates.

Sokrates, the man who places human reason above all, becomes the savior of Charmides. The name, Sokrates, is a contraction of *Soter*, meaning "Savior," and *Krates*, meaning "Mighty." Sokrates is the mighty savior of all who submit to him and the primacy of autonomous human reason above all. The word "autonomous" has an interesting derivation. It comes from two Greek words meaning "self" and "law." Sokrates, and all who follow his way, become laws unto themselves. The NAS hierarchy has become a law unto itself, answerable to no one. Their rule in the science classroom is a rule of self-proclaimed "experts." That "the wisdom of this world is stupidity with God" (I Corinthians 3:19) eludes them.

THE NAS' PHILOSOPHICAL SPELL

Just as Sokrates enchanted the youth, the NAS casts a spell to entrap the minds of its devotees. How does it work? It is not all that complicated, consisting as it does of three parts: a false promise, a taboo, and a threat. Let's look at them one at a time.

THE FALSE PROMISE: If you submit to our philosophical paradigm, then, along with us, relying on your mind, and your mind only, you can figure out all things, and solve the riddle of existence, including the origins of all life.

The promise is a philosophical appeal to human pride. Evo-atheist Michael Ruse says essentially the same thing in his book, *Darwinism Defended: A Guide to the Evolution Controversies*:

Darwinism, especially as it extends into human sociobiology, reflects a strong ideology. Moreover, this is one to be proud of. [1]

Just as becharmed philosophical apprenticeship under Sokrates supposedly is the cause of intellectual progress, so is submission to the NAS philosophers and their promise. The NAS hierarchy seeks those special people who are willing to submit:

This booklet is also directed to the broader audience of high-quality school and college students as well as adults who wish to become more familiar with the many strands of evidence supporting evolution and to understand why evolution is both a fact and a process that accounts for the diversity of life on Earth. (p. xii).

Students who, out of a combination of innocence and vanity, see themselves as part of humanity's elite—young princes and princesses of philosophy—yield their souls to the wisdom of the evo-atheist hierarchy, a prerequisite for the operation of the philosophical charm, or spell. The spirit behind the enchantment is beseeching, magical, and irrational. The entire NAS book is a rationalization of the enchantment, evoking the philosophical (seductive) power of the evo-atheist paradigm, making it seem so logical and so sensible that submissive scientists of imagined worm-descent will be able to unravel the mysteries of the universe. Thus, the NAS authorities successfully project their mere philosophical opinions into the minds of the enchanted as "facts." If that's not magic, what is it? Please don't forget that, ultimately, they target our children in the public schools through their multi-faceted seductions.

The NAS's false promise to its charmed ones is a variation of the ancient serpent's promise, "You shall be as gods, knowing good and evil." Genesis 3:6 tells us specifically what lured Eve:

And seeing is the woman that the tree is good for food, and that it brings a yearning to the eyes, and is to be coveted as the tree to make one intelligent (Genesis 3:6).

Remember in Chapter 1, we quoted NAS book committee member Neil deGrasse Tyson referring to the members of the NAS as "the most brilliant minds the nation has." That's what it is all about for them, taking the serpent's bait, and presuming themselves to be among the brilliant philosopher kings of science. Within their ivory towers, above their secluded and moated castles, they dispense the "wisdom" of human reptile-descent to the ignorant masses.

A voice from behind the idol-image of Apollo at Delphi called Sokrates "the wisest of men" (Apology 21a). Apollo took over Delphi from a python, and, as a result, Apollo's prophetess was called the Pythia. From within the Pythia emanated a "python spirit" (Acts 16:16). Thus it was the voice of a serpent that proclaimed Sokrates "the wisest of men." Whose idolatrous voice, I wonder, proclaims the NAS hierarchy to be the most brilliant of humans?

The Hebrew word for the serpent of Genesis comes from the primitive root, *nâchash*, meaning to hiss or whisper a magic spell. If you were to ask the evo-atheists if it is possible that they have been enchanted by the ancient serpent of Genesis, they would reply with a resounding "Never!" all the while insisting that they are descended from serpents.

The NAS writers use the word "overwhelming" over and over to support their empty presentation. It is my turn to use it: The overwhelming majority of today's evo-scientists, in truth pseudo-scientists, have fallen hook, line, and sinker for NAS's false promise— a false promise that is not all that unfamiliar to those of us who take the Book of Genesis seriously and literally.

THE TABOO: You are forbidden to think of, or mention, a Supreme Creator; likewise, you are forbidden to consider any involvement by such a Being in any aspect of the world.

The NAS writers express the taboo in their book thus:

. . . arguments that attempt to confuse students by suggesting that there are fundamental weaknesses in the science of evolution are unwarranted . . . (p. 52).

If we take out the dependent clauses, leaving just the subject and predicate, we have "arguments are unwarranted." The arguments to which they refer are coming from the creationists and those who espouse intelligent design. The NAS writers mean that creationist and intelligent design arguments are forbidden. That's the taboo.

Consider this sentence: "Because the evidence supporting it is so strong, scientists no longer question whether biological evolution has occurred and is continuing to occur." The key phrase: "scientists no longer question." The taboo again.

Consider this sentence also: "Others have argued that science teachers should 'teach the controversy' surrounding evolution. But there is no controversy in the scientific community about whether evolution has occurred." There can be no controversy so long as the taboo is not violated. Through this captivating taboo, the NAS hierarchy engraves its evo-atheistic viewpoint on the minds of the young and the eager, remaining immune to any criticism or debate. Submission to the philosophy of evo-atheism must be exclusive; thus the importance of blocking out the valid God hypothesis. The NAS hierarchy must be protected.

Last November, my friends, Mark Wadsworth, Mike Thompson, and I manned a booth at the Greek festival in Baltimore, Maryland. What a great time! On the third and final day, an evo-atheist from a college Classics department approached our display. He saw my books *Athena and Eden*, *Athena and Kain*, *The Parthenon Code: Mankind's History in Marble* (with "A Startling Testament to the Validity of Scripture" on the cover), and *Noah in Ancient Greek Art* with six Greek images of Noah on the cover. We also had a 950-slide PowerPoint show running, along with computer-reconstructed sculptures from the Parthenon and the temple of Zeus at Olympia. I tried to engage him as he looked over our display. He would have none of it. He raised his

75

hands, palms toward us, cried out, "No! No! No!," backed up, turned, and walked away. It was the taboo in operation.

If he had been rational, he'd have approached us and asked more about the evidence supporting our interpretation of ancient art, but the taboo is irrational, demanding denial instead of further investigation.

In 2003, the Institute for Creation Research published a 104-page "coffee table book" compiled by Tom Vail, a veteran tour guide, entitled *Grand Canyon: A Different View*. Vail's different view was a creationist one. The presidents of seven evo-science organizations cried in unison, "No! No! No!" urging the park superintendent to remove the book from Canyon bookstores because of its "religious" content. No one forced any gift shop visitors to buy Vail's book. In the United States of America, it is not rational to demand that non-obscene, non-defamatory books be removed from bookstores. The taboo made these evo-atheists express such an irrational demand.

THE THREAT: Unless you accept the taboo against postulating a Creator, and believe that you are capable of solving the riddle of existence, along with us, without reference to such a Being, you cannot be a scientist.

The threat completes the spell and magnifies the coercion inherent in the taboo. Both evince contempt for open-minded thinking. The threat is necessary to overcome the inability of the evo-atheists to make their case logically. They must revert to force. Because of their intellectual insecurity, they must take refuge in the irrational. Their spell is an essential aspect of their "scientific method."

Much of Ben Stein's new movie, *Expelled,* is about honest scientists who have followed evidence where it leads, and as a result, have found themselves fired and ostracized by the ruling evo-atheist hierarchy. Veiled threats abound: "You'll stay away from creationism and intelligent design if you know what's good for you." "Tenure is something we're happy to see happen for our *evolutionary* biologists." "Don't forget who pays your salary."

The spell has proven to be psychologically effective, destroying the spirit of discernment within those under it, and disabling their ability to independently and objectively evaluate evidence. Any objective scientist should be able to say without fear, "I can't prove that life evolved by chance through natural selection; therefore, there may be a Creator," but the evo-atheists cannot do this because of the philosophical enchantment which dominates their thinking.

The NAS's entire book is nothing more than the narration of an enchanting myth designed to persuade readers to favorably accept what the authors of it (the NAS hierarchy) say *should be believed*. Their evo-atheism is their philosophy of life first, and their philosophy of science second.

SOKRATES AND THE NAS: ENEMIES OF THE FAMILY AND THE STATE

Let's get back to Sokrates. Did he have anything of value to teach anyone? This is what Sarah Kofman, author of *Socrates: Fictions of a Philosopher*, has to say about him:

> . . . [I]n fact Socrates did not teach seriously. He did not adopt an edifying manner, he did not take the place of fathers or take over their responsibilities out of concern for their sons' welfare. With his disciples, his relationship was strictly negative: he did not communicate anything at all, nor did he satisfy, nor did he enrich. The corrupter of youth was a seducer, not only in the etymological sense of turning young people away from their families, but also in the modern sense which would make him first and foremost a tease . . . He gets young people excited when they are in contact with him, but he does not give them any strong, substantive nourishment. He abuses them, fascinates them, awakens nostalgic desires in them without satisfying them . . .[2]

A jury of Sokrates' peers convicted him of the charge of being "a doer of evil and corrupter of youth," and condemned him to death by drinking hemlock. The charge lay essentially in his encouragement of young people to disobey their parents. Today, this is exactly what the

NAS hierarchy encourages within our public school science classrooms.

Sane and responsible parents do not teach their children that they are descended from reptiles. Nor do they tell their children not to look to the heavens for their Maker, but rather to look down at the slimy, creeping things of the earth to discern their origins. And they do not desire that their children be tutored by atheists like Neil Tyson who proclaim that life has no meaning or purpose. Sokrates, 2400 years ago, was an alien and uninvited third party who presumed greater competence in the teaching of youth than the parents and everyone else. The hierarchy of the NAS, today, right now, is an uninvited third party in our public school science classrooms, presuming greater competence in teaching our children than we, the parents, and everyone else.

Sokrates was also convicted of impiety against the gods, a charge which pertained to his contempt for the average man and his love for dictatorship. Sokrates' jurors knew he didn't believe in free speech or democracy, but they did believe in those things. In his book, *The Trial of Socrates*, I. F. Stone argued that Sokrates was a coldhearted elitist snob, who favored totalitarian rule by an intellectual elite which he referred to as the "philosopher kings." Those who are a part of the hierarchy of the NAS imagine themselves as part of just such an elite. Like Sokrates, they lack respect for the family and the state.

THE CHIEF NAS PHILOSOPHER

The chilling enchantment of evo-atheist philosophy permeates the NAS to such a disturbing degree that you'd think the committee chair of the book project, Francisco J. Ayala, was a philosophy professor at a major university. He is, indeed, just such a professor.

Francisco Jose Ayala (born 1934) is Professor of Philosophy, (School of Humanities), and Professor of Logic and the Philosophy of Science (School of Social Sciences) at the University of California, Irvine. He is also Professor of Biological Sciences, Ecology and Evolutionary Biology (School of Biological Sciences). Ayala moved to the United States in 1961 from his home-city of Madrid to attend Columbia University, where he studied for his doctorate under Theodosius Dobzhansky, graduating in 1964.

Ayala's studies under Dobzhansky shed much light on the core philosophical problem at the National Academy of Sciences. Dobzhansky is the one who wrote "Nothing in biology makes sense except in the light of evolution." This is not an objective scientific statement, but rather a philosophical one. It defines Dobzhansky's and Ayala's philosophy of science—the same fallacious philosophy of science Ayala and the NAS are foisting on every public school student in America. You most likely had never heard of Dobzhansky or Ayala before reading this book, and yet your children must go along with their bogus philosophical presumptions or fail in science class.

The truth is that "Nothing in biology makes sense except in light of the evidence, the data, the facts!" Let me re-emphasize: "the evidence, the data, the facts!" That is what true science is based upon. And the facts do not point to humanity's descent from reptiles.

Note that Ayala is a professor of logic. Fundamental errors in logic abound in the NAS book, the writing of which was overseen by Ayala. And did you read the previous chapter about the Clergy Letter Project? There are enough logical errors in that letter alone to fill a month of days in your diary, and yet Ayala touts it as something reasonable and good! Ayala and his 18-member committee that oversaw the writing of the NAS book are completely out of hand, their thinking disconnected from reality. The inmates are running the asylum.

The following quotes are from Ayala's book *Darwin and Intelligent Design*:

There is probably no other notion in any field of science that has been as extensively tested and as thoroughly corroborated as the evolutionary origin of living organisms. (p. 40).

It is now possible to assert that gaps of knowledge in the evolutionary history of living organisms no longer exist . . . The virtually unlimited evolutionary information encoded in the DNA sequence of living

organisms allows evolutionists to reconstruct all evolutionary relationships leading to present-day organisms, with as much detail as desired. (p. 41).

The missing link is no longer missing. Hundreds of fossil remains belonging to hundreds of intermediate human ancestors have been discovered since Darwin's time and continue to be discovered at an accelerated rate. (p. 43).

All three quotes above are absolutely false. I have as much evidence for: "There are five-eyed chartreuse aliens on the dark side of the moon preparing to pelt us with sweet potatoes" as Ayala has for his statements. Ayala's words are not those of a truth-seeking scientist, but rather the rantings of an evo-atheist lunatic. They show us that the more exalted the philosopher, the grander the delusion. Ayala's words *seem* true only when they are artificially and arbitrarily glued to his bogus philosophy of science. These evo-atheists who run the NAS are not teachers of knowledge; they are rather, like Sokrates, antidemocratic reactionaries.

The men and women who put the NAS book together, and the rest of the NAS hierarchy, are unable to comprehend the enormous difference between *saying* something is true, and *proving* that it is true. While such a handicap has no bearing upon their respective abilities to philosophize, it categorically disqualifies them as competent scientists.

We began Chapter 3 by citing Colossians 2:8-9:

Beware that no one shall be despoiling you through philosophy and empty seduction, in accord with human tradition, in accord with the elements of the world, and not in accord with Christ, for in Him the entire complement of the Deity is dwelling bodily.

We've seen in this Chapter and in the three which preceded it, that what sustains the evo-atheists of the National Academy of Sciences is not evidence for their position, but rather "philosophy and empty seduction," just as the scriptural passage maintains.

We'll see in the next two chapters that the adamant reliance of the NAS members on philosophy and empty seduction necessitates their violation of our most cherished political principles.

CHAPTER 7

Violating the First Amendment: Religion

Congress shall make no law respecting an establishment of religion, or prohibiting the free exercise thereof; or abridging the freedom of speech, or of the press; or the right of the people peaceably to assemble, and to petition the government for a redress of grievances.

Amendment I to the Constitution of the United States of America

BELIEF IN EVOLUTION REQUIRES AN ENORMOUS AMOUNT OF FAITH

We saw in Chapter 3 that the NAS admits in its book that they have no evidence whatsoever for how matter turned into life. They do, however, speculate wildly about it in the following paragraph from page 22 of their book. I have italicized the iffy words and phrases:

. . . researchers have shown how this process *might have* worked by studying a molecule known as RNA. Researchers recently discovered that some RNA molecules *can* greatly increase the rate of specific chemical reactions, including the replication of parts of other RNA molecules. *If* a molecule like RNA *could* reproduce itself (*perhaps* with the assistance of other molecules), it *could* form the basis for a very simple living organism. *If* such self-replicators were packaged within chemical vesicles or membranes, they *might have* formed "protocells"—early versions of very simple cells. Changes in these molecules *could lead* to variants that, for example, replicated more efficiently in a particular environment. In this way, natural selection *would* begin to operate, creating opportunities for protocells that had advantageous molecular innovations to increase in complexity.

When I read in the second chapter of Genesis that God makes Adam "of soil from the ground, and He is blowing into his nostrils the breath of the living, and becoming is the human a living soul," I find it very easy to believe. On the other hand, evolutionists, in order to believe their above paragraph, have some extraordinary faith-stretching to do. Their paragraph is written entirely in the subjunctive—the mood which presents the molecular events not as factual, but as contingent, possible, and doubtful. It *might* have happened, *perhaps*, *if*. The point is that their views constitute a belief-system, an extremely far-fetched belief system at that. They *believe* that their above speculation is a reasonable explanation for the origin of life. Faith in molecules-to-man evolution, absent evidence for it, is a belief-system. It is thus religious in essence.

Happiness is one of the emotions. Its opposite, unhappiness, also falls under the category of emotions. Likewise, since theism is a belief-system or religion, its opposite, atheism, also falls under the category of a belief-system or religion.

Within the framework of their own book, they define themselves as embracing a religious belief. They write on page 50:

. . . an important component of religious belief is faith, which implies acceptance of a truth regardless of the presence of empirical evidence for or against that truth.

Do they accept as one of their "truths" that life spontaneously generated itself from matter through the operation of natural selection—"regardless of the presence of empirical evidence for or against that truth"? Yes, they do. Ergo, hence, and therefore, evo-atheism is a religious belief. They say quite correctly that "an important component of religious belief is faith." How do the evo-atheists make up for the fact that they don't have a stitch of evidence to put into the bushel baskets? They make up for it with their remarkable faith. Let's go even deeper into this rich faith of theirs—because it surely is not science. And why isn't it science? Because as the NAS writers say on page 12 of their book, ". . . science is a way of knowing that differs

84

from other ways in its *dependence on empirical evidence . . .*" (my emphasis). No empirical evidence, no science.

NATURAL SELECTION AS THE GOD OF ATHEIST EVOLUTION

We saw in Chapter 2 that "natural selection" is, first and foremost, a figure of speech, and that the NAS writers define it three different ways. It is the "driving force" of evolution. They also describe it as a "process," and as an outcome ("reproductive success"). Natural selection is a driving force, a process, and an end result.

In my faith, Jesus is the "way." In evo-atheism, Natural Selection is the way, or process (I'm capitalizing the phrase for the rest of this chapter out of respect for their religion). In my faith, Jesus is the "Alpha and Omega," the "First and the Last." In the faith of evo-atheism, Natural Selection is the first and the last—the driving force and the outcome.

In the Hebrew Scriptures, Yahweh is one of the names of the Supreme Creator God. Pertaining to His mastery over all time, it means basically "Is-Becoming-Will Be." Natural Selection in a sense imitates the meaning of Yahweh's Name with its "driving force-process-outcome." On page 6 of their book, the NAS writes that Natural Selection "can have radically different evolutionary effects over different timescales." Natural Selection is a god of time who accounts for everything in nature.

The NAS's made-up account of the beginning of life, cited at the beginning of this chapter, gives us even more insight into the imaginary "awesome power" of Natural Selection. Please read their fanciful paragraph again. As you do so, you will note that even after they force all the necessary, preposterous contingencies into place, still no life emerges. But then, Natural Selection shows up on the scene, "creating opportunities for protocells" to come alive. This is the evo-atheist version of God breathing life into Adam. Yea and verily, Natural Selection, that astonishing and worthy figure of speech, hath created life. From this point on, Natural Selection a "driving force" takes over, then Natural Selection a "process" moves in, and finally Natural Selection an outcome rules. Three Natural Selections in One Natural Selection. Natural Selection, that oh-so-venerable figure of speech, turns out to be very similar to the obtuse mystery of the Roman Catholic Trinity as Thomas Aquinas described it in his *Summa Theologica*.

We are enthusiastic Maryland Terrapin basketball fans around here. In the years around the team's national championship season, they had a player who could make lay-ups, hit three-pointers, pass off, get rebounds, play defense, and fire up the team. We used to say that he was everywhere and could do it all. Some people used to say they saw him in the stands at halftime, hawking beer and peanuts to the fans.

The NAS writers claim that Natural Selection is everywhere and can do it all, too. But their pet notion is not at all like our favorite Terp basketball player—whose abilities were real. In truth, Natural Selection is nowhere and does nothing. It is just a figure of speech employed by atheists so that they don't have to acknowledge or give thanks to their Creator.

NATURAL SELECTION AS A MYSTICAL, MIRACULOUS, SUPERNATURAL FORCE

The NAS writers acknowledge on page 54 of their book that "many religious beliefs involve entities or ideas that currently are not within the domain of science." What they refuse to acknowledge is that their be-all and do-all, Natural Selection, is just such an entity or idea. The evo-atheists call it a "driving force"—a force that cannot be measured, and which appears to be without measure. If Jesus, Who has been given the Spirit of God without measure (John 3:34), possesses supernatural aspects, so then does Natural Selection in their religious scheme.

Natural Selection is omnipresent. It operates upon every flora population in South America, upon all the rat populations in Asia, and upon the tsetse fly populations in Africa—all at the same time. From the evo-atheist standpoint, without Natural Selection, there can be no life. Jesus said, "I am the Way and the Truth and the Life." The evo-atheists of the NAS believe that Natural Selection is the way and the truth and the life. Without it, chaos reigns, and so it becomes, for the evo-atheists, the central organizing principle of all life, including human consciousness. The Scriptures teach that by God and through Christ, all things consist (Colossians 1:15-17). The evo-atheists believe that by evolution through Natural Selection, all living things consist.

Natural Selection's reality is neither apparent to the senses nor obvious to the intelligence, and its character is profoundly inexplicable. This makes it mystical.

No law of Natural Selection has ever been formulated. According to the evo-atheists, it is a force, a process, and a result in the physical world deviating from the known laws of nature, actually transcending our knowledge of these laws. The NAS writers' description of life coming into being through the "creative power" of Natural Selection is nothing less than the description of a miracle. We've seen in Chapter 4 that the NAS writers cannot intelligibly explain how Natural Selection accounts for irreducibly complex systems in nature, yet they still insist that in some unrevealed way, it can. This is mysticism, and perhaps, another miracle. Natural Selection, as the evo-atheists themselves describe it, is both miraculous and supernatural.

EVO-ATHEISTS URGE FAITH IN THEIR SCIENCE

According to Scripture, "faith is an assumption of what is being expected, a conviction concerning matters which are not being observed" (Hebrews 11:1). So it is also with the evolutionists. The spontaneous chemical generation of life from matter, the evolution of the sexes, and speciation never have been observed, yet evo-atheists have faith in all three. While Christians have faith in what God will do in the future, the evo-atheists put their faith in what science will do:

The history of science shows that even very difficult questions such as how life originated may become amenable to solution as a result of

advances in theory, the development of new instrumentation and the discovery of new facts. (p. 22).

EVO-ATHEISTS ADMIT THE REALITY OF THEIR RELIGION

We've seen that some evo-atheists are very straightforward about what their evo-atheism really is. Richard Dawkins titled the first chapter of his book *The God Delusion*, "A Deeply Religious Believer in No God." Sir Julian Huxley called evolution "religion without revelation." Cornell University professor, Will Provine, wrote that one can have a religious view compatible with evolution "only if the religious view is indistinguishable from atheism." Leading biologist and evolutionist, Lynn Margulis, disapproves of the uncritical belief by many of her colleagues in Natural Selection thus:

The Darwinian claim to explain all of evolution is a popular half-truth whose lack of explicative power is compensated for only by the religious ferocity of its rhetoric.[1]

Indeed, the NAS hierarchy pushes its evo-atheistic religion in the classroom with "ferocity," and with a zeal that's hardly matched in Christianity. We can't properly call them evangelical, however, because that word comes from the Greek *eu-angellion*, meaning literally, *well-message*, more commonly, *good news*. Teaching children or adults that they are descended from reptiles is never good news. We should call evo-atheists *mal-angelical*, because it accurately describes what they're doing: spreading hopelessly bad *religious* news.

THE NAS VIOLATES THE ESTABLISHMENT CLAUSE OF THE FIRST AMENDMENT

The National Academy of Sciences has had a mandate from Congress since 1863 to advise the federal government on issues of science and technology, and that's all. What are they doing coming into all of our elementary schools, all of our junior highs, and all of our high schools with a disguised demand that our children embrace their evo-atheism? What are they doing teaching our children that they are descended from worms and reptiles? What are they doing imposing their atheistic religious faith on our children when we're not around? What are they doing sowing atheism in our schools?

On page 52 of their book, the NAS writers say that "arguments that attempt to confuse students by suggesting that there are fundamental weaknesses in the science of evolution are unwarranted . . ." Unwarranted means unauthorized. Criticism of evo-atheism in the science classroom is currently unauthorized.

Could the U.S. Congress pass a constitutional law saying that, in the science classroom, only the evo-atheist religious viewpoint is acceptable? No way. It would be a violation of the establishment clause of the First Amendment. Yet, based on the situation in our public school classrooms today, such a menacing law may as well have been passed already. The effect is the same, and that's what matters. Evo-atheists have imposed their own religious viewpoint, and established it as the only authorized one throughout all the public school science classrooms in America.

There is no question that belief in evolution requires a huge amount of religious faith, and that Natural Selection is their miraculous, mystical, and supernatural god. Sokrates worshipped Pan, the god of nature. The evo-atheists of the NAS worship that same god under the name, Natural Selection.

We've seen that the big wigs among the evo-atheists admit that their views constitute a religious outlook. Ironically, their own words on page 45 of their book condemn their adamant insistence that their religious dogma must dominate the minds of students in the science classroom:

. . . [A]s civil servants, public school teachers must be neutral with respect to religion, which means that they can neither promote nor inhibit its practice . . . Because the Constitution of the United States forbids a federal establishment of religion, it would be inappropriate to use public

funds to teach the views of just one religion or one religious subgroup to all students.

But the atheistic hypocrites at the NAS won't let that happen without a bitter fight. They realize that yielding on any point—the fact that they have no evidence for evolution, that they cannot honestly explain irreducible complexity, or that they have no business sowing atheism in the classroom—will lead to an opening of the flood gates, and that deluge will ultimately wash their evo-atheist religion and their phony "factual theory" down the sewer where it belongs.

While the NAS book promotes primarily its own evo-atheist religion in the science classroom, it also promotes as acceptable any other religion that accepts evo-science. This is a violation of the establishment of religion clause of the First Amendment as well. The twisted logic begins here as they write, "Attempts to pit science and religion against each other create controversy where none needs to exist" (p. 12). Then they define an acceptable religion, as noted in Chapter 5, as one that accepts evo-atheism. We find another disguised tautology here. What they are really saying is that there need be no controversy between evo-science and religious groups that accept evo-science. As soon as every religion accepts evo-science, no controversy at all will remain, because evo-science gets along so well with itself! Remember, the committee chairman of the NAS book project, Francisco J. Ayala, is a professor of (can you believe it?) logic.

In direct reply to the mastermind behind this transparent tautology and to the rest of the deceptions in his book, let me say, "Likewise, Professor Ayala, there need be no controversy between my belief in the absolute truth of the Scriptures and the beliefs of others—so long as they also believe in the absolute truth of the Scriptures."

THE RELIGIOUS UNTOUCHABLES ACCORDING TO THE NAS

Speaking of the Scriptures, who are the religious groups that will not get on board the NAS peace train? The NAS book singles out essentially just one group:

Religious denominations that do not accept the occurrence of evolution tend to be those that believe in strictly literal interpretations of religious texts. (p. 12).

With a single sentence, they try to dismiss the tens of millions of us (it wouldn't matter if it were only ten of us) who believe the claim the Bible makes of itself—that it is the true and inspired Word of the Creator God. But instead of dismissing us, their language lends credence to the creationist position. The primary meaning of "literal" is "true" or "truthful." While I and many others believe in strictly *true* interpretations of religious texts, Zimmerman, Mr. X, and all the other evo-atheists must embrace strictly *false* interpretations of religious texts. Every *true* interpretation of Scripture—God's Word—is like hot acid on the evo-atheist's thin skin.

The writers of the NAS book cannot be honest and say what they mean: "We are atheists, and to us, by definition, the Bible is false. Do not take any of its passages literally; that is, do not take any of its passages 'as truthful,' if you expect to learn our brand of science and prosper in it."

CHAPTER 8

Violating the First Amendment: Free Speech

As I read the NAS's book, *Science, Evolution, and Creationism* for the first time, I had a feeling of déjà vu. After the second and third readings, it was just as Yogi Berra had said, "Déjà vu all over again." The illegal banning of my welfare fraud board game by government-directed action back in the 1980s kept popping into my mind. It is a very controversial game, you may have heard of it. It is called *Public Assistance: Why Bother Working for a Living?*

On the third reading of the NAS book, I could see plainly that it shared all the anti-free speech elements of the illegal, yet successful, nationwide plan to "remove the [welfare] game from the marketplace." A review of that situation in the 1980s will prove to be instructive for comparison to what the NAS is doing in the American science classroom today. After a two-and-a-half-page introduction to the game, I will interject comments every so often, using parentheses and a different font, about how the NAS's efforts to ban the God hypothesis correspond to the banning of the game.

PLAYING THE WELFARE GAME

Ron Pramschufer, the co-inventor of the game, and I intended it to be a parody of government liberalism, with a special focus on the able-bodied loaferism, welfare fraud, and the social chaos its domestic policies promote. The object for the players of the game is to accumulate as much money as possible in twelve circuits around the board, each lap representing a month, as they move back and forth between the "Able-bodied Welfare Recipient's Promenade" and the "Working Person's Rut."

93

The able-bodied welfare recipient collects money through such methods as having out-of-wedlock children, playing the lottery and the horses, drawing "Welfare Benefit" cards, stealing hubcaps, and making profitable side trips into the four "Saturday Night" crimes: drug dealing, gambling, prostitution, and armed robbery.

Players unfortunate enough to land on one of the "Get a Job" blocks have to move out of the Welfare Promenade and into the Working Person's Rut. There, they usually experience an unending series of bills, meager paychecks, discrimination, welfare taxes, and other assorted "Working Person's Burdens."

Both able-bodied loafers and those in the Working Person's Rut have opportunities to land a high-pay/no-work job for their other playing piece, representing their live-in or spouse, on the "Government Cakewalk." To portray the American reality, we made it so that the only way a player's live-in or spouse can be removed from the lucrative Cakewalk is to land on the square that says, "You are conscience-stricken. Quit government job."

The "Jail Jaunt" rounds out the socialist reality represented by the game. Able-bodied loafers turned Saturday night criminals must move there if they get caught in one of their illegal acts. Players in the Working Person's Rut do not experience the Jail Jaunt, because they are too busy or too tired to engage in criminal activity. The Jail Jaunt, as most of the rest of the game, typifies the reality of liberal government policies: one roll—"Lawyer gets you off on technicality," for example—and you're right back at the welfare office ready to collect all benefits and resume your strut on the welfare promenade.

The winner is the one with the most money at the end of twelve months, and chances are, unless you can get off that Working Person's Rut and back on the Able-Bodied Welfare Recipient's Promenade, it isn't going to be you.

The game wasn't meant as a 100% accurate and thorough critique of American social policy, but as a lampoon. The research for it consisted of television and newspaper reports, observations and conversations, and one visit to a local Maryland welfare office where an administrator was very candid with us.

Our spoof was based on street knowledge and common sense. Ron and I saw ourselves more as packaging experts than game inventors. We often told people, "We didn't invent this game; government liberals did. We just put it in a box."

We designed the package for the impulse buy in high traffic locations, and we felt we had a large, natural market for the game with everybody's "Uncle Charlie" or "Aunt Bea" who complained about welfare. We expected some criticism, certainly, but not much more than a political cartoonist might receive. There are more than 5,000 words in the game. It is provocative political opinion, words and ideas supposedly protected by the First Amendment.

Inasmuch as the game deals with welfare chiselers, able-bodied loafers, and liberal government bureaucrats who tolerate and encourage massive welfare fraud across the United States, the game met with much media attention.

In the fall of 1980, Ron and I, like most Americans at that time and even today, had never heard of The American Public Welfare Association (APWA)—the nerve center of America's welfare empire. (They have since changed their name to The American Public Human Services Association, or APHSA, but I will continue to refer to them as the APWA). Its board of directors is made up mostly of the welfare commissioners of state and local welfare agencies. The APWA pushes relentlessly for expansion of the empire and what it calls its "progressive" agenda by skewing welfare data to make it look like more funding is always needed, by manipulating bills through various Congressional committees, by translating welfare laws into the welfare rules that the various executive agencies use to dole out government largess, and by propagandizing in the media. When the APWA meets public opposition in a certain program, it holds its ground there, while pushing hard to expand other welfare programs not under public scrutiny. The majority of its budget comes from taxes in the form of dues which the state and local welfare agencies pay annually. The

APWA bureaucrats who run the welfare empire are not elected by the public; they are not even appointed by elected officials. They elect themselves.

(The members of the NAS hierarchy aren't popularly elected either. They don't respect what the public thinks except in the sense that they want to manipulate and control public thinking in order to further their evo-atheist agenda.)

The APWA controls the National Council of State Public Welfare Administrators (changed in 1997 to the National Council of State Human Service Administrators) and the National Council of Local Public Welfare Administrators (changed in 1997 to the National Council of Local Human Service Administrators). Its affiliate groups include The American Association of Public Welfare Attorneys, the American Association of Public Welfare Information Systems Management, the Association of Food Stamp Directors, and the State Medicaid Directors' Association.

(The NAS spreads its atheist tentacles through the Council of the National Academy of Sciences, People for the American Way, the National Center for Science Education, the Institute of Medicine, the American Association for the Advancement of Science, the National Science Teachers Association, the Biotechnology Institute, the various state academies of science, hundreds of colleges and universities, and many other evo-atheist organizations.)

"PROPERLY EDUCATING" THE PUBLIC

In the fall of 1980, the APWA was riding high on the waves of unprecedented welfare expansion. Its leaders had become sophisticated propagandists. In its November newsletter, the APWA interviewed its treasurer, Jerome Chapman, who was also the welfare commissioner of Texas. The article concluded thus:

Chapman notes that administrators have only just begun the task of educating the public so that it understands and supports public welfare. He believes usually overlooked but potential allies in this endeavor are business and industry. He notes that certain industries benefit directly from welfare programs, e.g., food chains from food stamps and the medical profession from Medicaid. And businesses that sell the necessities of life, such as clothing, rental housing, and utilities would find higher benefit levels in programs such as aid to families with dependent children (AFDC) to their advantage.

In Texas, one member of the commissioner's staff spends part of his time helping corporations understand how welfare programs work. Chapman believes that once corporations are won over, they can be enlisted to help sell the public on the welfare system.

("Properly educating" the American public is the aim of the NAS as well. In the process, they've become very sophisticated propagandists. Their influential allies, themselves thoroughly propagandized by the NAS, include the editors of *National Geographic, Discovery, Science, Scientific American, Time, Nature, U.S. News and World Report, and Newsweek* magazines, as well as the editors of the major daily newspapers in America. PBS and the History, Discovery, and Science channels also report their "science" under the Darwinist journalistic paradigm: evolution is always assumed, never proven; and creationism is always denied, never refuted.

The focus of the NAS is, of course, "properly educating" science teachers, principals, and school boards about their descent from reptiles.)

PRESIDENT REAGAN NOT CONSIDERED A THREAT TO WELFARE EMPIRE'S GOALS

The APWA did not consider the election of Ronald Reagan in November of 1980 to be a real threat to its power because its leaders knew that they could push their programs through a democratic Congress. And this they did. Back in the early eighties, the public may have been fed a chorus of complaints about the Reagan administration's so-called brutal cuts in welfare, but in reality, from

97

1980 to 1983 the total cost of the top five welfare programs rose 37%, from $42.8 billion to $58.6 billion.

(Like the APWA, the National Academy of Sciences operates within its field with impunity, with no significant Congressional oversight. The House Science and Technology Committee ought to be holding hearings right now on why the NAS insists the creationist hypothesis must be banned from science classes, and why the only acceptable hypothesis is the empty atheistic evolutionary one.)

GAME POPULARITY SCARED WELFARE BIG WIGS

The APWA's leaders felt threatened by the game, by the publicity it was receiving, and by its growing popularity. Once Ron and I had the first copies of the game in our hands in October of 1980, we took one to the Annapolis Evening Capital newspaper, and the editors ran a front page story on it. The Associated Press picked it up and made it front page news across the country. After that, Ron and I were asked to appear on several nationwide radio and television talk shows including *The Donahue Show*. The publicity generated calls for the game to toy and gift stores, and these retailers turned to their manufacturer's representatives to locate the game, and these, in turn, ordered the game from us. We were well on our way to establishing a successful marketing network across the country.

The press just kept getting better. New York Daily News reporter Edward J. Fay quoted a Macy's worker in a full page article, "Everyone's asking for it, but we don't have it yet." *Giftware News* called it "the most original game of the decade if not the century," and wrote of "overwhelming support from major metropolitan department store customers." The *Donahue* producers had to hire a new person to handle all the calls for the game after we appeared on his ten minute segment of *The Today Show*. It was about this time that the welfare empire potentates determined that the game *Public Assistance—Why Bother Working for a Living?* had to be removed from the marketplace of ideas.

98

(The banning of the welfare game and the attempt to keep the God hypothesis out of public school science classrooms both involve a clash between elitist bureaucracies and everyday citizens who want what is their natural right—open and free access to all opinions. A 2006 Zogby Poll revealed that about 70% percent of Americans believe that scientific criticism of evolution should be included in public schools. The NAS cannot tolerate that, any more than the APWA could tolerate wide-spread criticism of their welfare policy in the form of a board game.)

In a speech before the National Association of Broadcasters, President Jimmy Carter's head of Health and Human Services, Patricia Roberts Harris, spoke out against the game. Fearful of the effect of its continued sale on welfare empire expansion policy, she called it "racist and sexist" and urged the media not to give it any more publicity.

There is no basis whatsoever to the claim that the game is racist and sexist. Racism and sexism are just not part of the game, period. You can check the game board, the rules, and sample Welfare Benefit and Working Person's Burden cards for yourself at welfaregame.com. The APWA's intent in this vile, oft-repeated, name-calling was to brand us as ignorant and ill-motivated people.

(The writers of the NAS book have a similar intent when it comes to creationists, portraying us—for embracing a viable scientific hypothesis that they despise for philosophical and religious reasons—as stupid, non-scientific, narrow-minded religious fanatics. When presidential candidate, Mike Huckabee, revealed he was a creationist, University of Michigan professor Gilbert Omenn, one of the authors of the NAS book, said he would "worry that a president who didn't believe in evolution arguments" would also, for instance, disregard evidence that smoking cigarettes is unhealthy. "This is a way of leading our country to ruin," Omenn told reporters. The head of the NAS book committee, Francisco Ayala, put creationists and witches in the same category: "We don't teach witchcraft as an alternative to medicine. We must not teach creationism as an alternative to evolution," he said.)

Meanwhile, privately, other leaders of the welfare empire worked on the specifics of the plan to ban the game nationwide. Peter Slavin, the editor of the APWA's monthly newsletter, was one of those leaders. He wrote in his notes as he helped prepare the plan, "Game could be very harmful . . . Game will reinforce moves to cut public assistance . . . Will create backlash toward social service programs as a whole and welfare in particular." The head of the New York City welfare agency admitted under oath that he worked along with the APWA to get the game off the market because he didn't want the state legislature to see the game, fearing it might not increase welfare grants as he had requested.

(It is all about money and power. A science classroom open to the God hypothesis and other threatening ideas, will lead to much embarrassment for the NAS, a loss of prestige, and most important, a loss of the money associated with that prestige.)

Slavin and the APWA's executive director, Edward Weaver, based their nationwide plan to ban the game on the successful efforts of Maryland officials who worked with the NAACP and other welfare "rights" groups to keep the game off shelves there, and upon a plan already implemented by the National Organization for Women (NOW). After speaking with Maryland welfare officials and officials from NOW, Slavin wrote in his notes, "Yes, good chance of organized opposition being successful . . . Opponents need to contact stores directly, bring economic pressure."

(The pressure the NAS brings is of a different sort, relying on their authority as "experts" in science, threatening that the abandonment of evo-science will lead to a return to the Dark Ages. In their book, the NAS writers make the outrageous assertion that without evo-science, counteracting threatening viruses with antibiotic resistance would be impossible. The reality is that molecules-to-man evolution has nothing to do with that at all.

NAS propagandist, Paul A. Hanle, president of the NAS-affiliated Biotechnology Institute, carries this scare tactic to the extreme. He has written in nationally published editorials that teaching human evolution from reptiles is essential for solving "food-related and environmental problems," necessary to "combat the spread of AIDS, biowarfare and pandemic diseases, [and] to give us lifesaving new cures and life-improving new breakthroughs."

Hanle opined in *The Washington Post*:

The opposition to evolution discourages the development of entire high-school classes of future scientific talent. "It seems like a raw deal for the 14-year-old girl in Topeka who might have gone on to find a cure for resistant infections if only she had been taught evolution in high school," H. Holden Thorp, chairman of the chemistry department at the University of North Carolina at Chapel Hill, wrote in the New York Times last spring.

Hanle, the Chicken Little of evo-atheism, goes so far as to say that opposing evolution "could decimate the development of U.S. scientific talent and erode whatever competitive advantage the United States enjoys in the technology-based global economy." The APWA implies that unless their funding demands are met, millions of children will starve. Hanle and the NAS imply that unless we teach our children we're all descended from reptiles, we'll become a third-rate power overnight. This is fear-mongering of the most despicable sort. If you want a good laugh, read his articles in full at biotechinstitute.org. His ideas are as well-thought out as those in the Clergy Project Letter.)

THE GOVERNMENT PLAN TO "REMOVE THE GAME FROM THE MARKETPLACE"

The APWA first sent its plan to ban the welfare game on November 19th, 1980 to the welfare "CEO's of states" [their term] in the form of an "action alert," then to all members of the APWA, about 10,000 in number, including all state and local welfare agencies from the Virgin Islands to Alaska and from Maine to Hawaii, in its December, 1980 newsletter, Washington Report. This is what it said:

An Open Letter to All APWA Members from Executive Director Edward T. Weaver.

I am writing this letter to alert you to a new board game entitled, "Public Assistance—Why Bother Working for a Living?". This game is described in the accompanying article.

I agree with Secretary [of Health and Human Services Patricia] Harris, the NAACP, and the National Organization for Women that the game is callous, racist, sexist, and a "vicious brand of stereotyping." We, who are part of the reality of public welfare, understand the myths that surround the work we do and the people we serve. This game, however, plays out the basest forms of this mythology; we must not let it go unchallenged. I encourage you, as concerned APWA members, to take the following course of action:

1. Do an informal survey to see if the game is being sold in your area. If it is not, keep a watchful eye and initiate the actions in No. 2 below if it appears. You may be able to join with others to contact store owners/managers to discourage buying.

2. If the game is available in your area:

a. Don't buy it yourself. Let your friends know it is not a "cute" holiday gift.

b. Spread the word to other interested groups (welfare rights advocates, civil rights groups, and women's groups).

c. Either alone or in combination with the groups identified in "b" contact the store owner manager and/or buyer to explain why the game is offensive and should not be carried.

d. Keep us informed of your efforts

As executive director of the American Public Welfare Association, I feel an obligation to you and to the mission we commonly serve to alert you to the "Public Assistance" game and to suggest the course of action I have outlined. If there are any questions that I, or APWA staff, can answer for you or information that we can share, please do not hesitate to contact us.

We at APWA headquarters will be doing what we can, in conjunction with our Washington colleagues, to remove the game from the marketplace.

It was a brilliant, government-directed, publicly-financed plan, utilizing all of the intimidating power of the political left. In practice, the plan was designed to go like this: first, the local welfare empire official calls or writes to the store president or owner and expresses "concern" that the game just might not be in good taste or in the best interests of poor people. Next, representatives of the NAACP call or drop by unannounced and demand to know how the store can conceivably consider carrying a "racist" game. They threaten the store with a boycott and negative publicity. If the store has not caved in by this time, representatives of NOW pay a visit and demand to know how the store could consider carrying such a "racist" and "sexist" item. They threaten endless phone calls and picketing, and noise in the street at the store entrance.

Central to the plan to ban the game is the idea that, if the American voter and taxpayer is offered a choice between welfare "mythology" as expressed in the game and welfare "reality" as espoused by the bureaucrats, he or she will mindlessly embrace the welfare "mythology" of the game, and be thus tricked by a couple of guys from Maryland into opposing welfare expansion. Let me put that another way: implicit in the efforts to ban the game is the elitist bureaucratic notion that the American people are too stupid to know which games are worthy of their own independent purchase and which are not; therefore, the game, *Public Assistance—Why Bother Working for a Living?*, had to be forced out of the marketplace for the good of the taxpayers themselves!

(The same things are true about the NAS' plan to keep the discussion of creationism out of the classroom. If the students are allowed to hear arguments in favor of creationism, they might be mindlessly drawn into believing that it makes more sense than evolution. The underlying idea is that science teachers and students are not qualified to evaluate evidence on their own. One Maryland welfare official said about *Public Assistance*, "This is a game the American people are better off not knowing about." The writers of the NAS book don't say it outright, but they infer throughout, "Evidence for creationism and the God hypothesis are things that American students and science teachers are better off not knowing about."

Bureaucratic thugs think alike. All we have to do is make a few key changes in the APWA's censorship plan, and we have the essence of the NAS plan to keep the God hypothesis out of public school science classrooms:

An Open Letter to All Public School Science Teachers from Ralph J. Cicerone, President, National Academy of Sciences.

I am writing to alert you to a very dangerous idea now being circulated in some science classrooms known as the God Hypothesis. The falsity and dangers to us of the spread of this idea are described in the accompanying booklet.

I agree with Neil Tyson, Richard Dawkins, the ACLU, the Institute of Medicine, the Darwin Day organizers, and the signers of the Clergy Letter Project that this God Hypothesis is anti-science, the work of religious fanatics, and a vicious brand of science misrepresentation. We, who are part of atheistic evolutionary science, understand the myths that surround the work we do, and the students and teachers we serve. This God Hypothesis plays out the basest form of this mythology.

I encourage you, as concerned science teachers and advocates for evolutionary atheism, to take the following course of action:

1. Do an informal survey to see if this God Hypothesis is being expressed in any of the schools in your county. If it is not, keep a watchful eye and initiate the actions in No. 2 below if you hear of any mention of it. You may be able to join with others to contact educators and school boards to discourage the expression of the God Hypothesis.

If the God Hypothesis is being expressed in the schools in your area:

a. Do not listen to explanations of it yourself. Let your friends know that it is not a "cute" idea to discuss the merits of the God Hypothesis.

b. Spread the word to other interested groups (the ACLU, the Clergy Letter Project, and humanist societies in your area).

c. Either alone or in combination with the groups identified in "b" contact the principal and school board overseeing the school in violation of our educational policy. Explain why the God Hypothesis is offensive and should not be expressed.

d. Keep us informed of your efforts.

As president of the National Academy of Sciences, I feel an obligation to you and the mission we commonly serve to alert you to the dangers of the God Hypothesis being expressed, and suggest the course of action I have outlined. If there are any questions that I, or the NAS staff, can answer for you or information that we can share, please do not hesitate to contact us.

We at the NAS headquarters will be doing what we can, in conjunction with our Washington colleagues, to remove the God Hypothesis from all science classrooms, and from the larger marketplace of ideas.)

THE CENSORSHIP MENTALITY OF THE NAS

Those who worked to ban the game fit in the historical matrix with those who, in order to retain power, drew up the Alien and Sedition Acts; with those who, throughout the Southern States, passed laws restricting the press, speech, and discussion regarding slavery, and who made it a crime to merely possess abolitionist literature—so that their unjust economic system of involuntary servitude might prevail; and with those who jailed anti-war speaker Eugene Debs to keep him quiet. Those who forced the game off the market stepped beyond these three historical illustrations because, although those perpetrators were dreadfully wrong, they at least followed due process. Those who worked to ban the game did not act in accord with any law, good or bad: they acted above the law, as a law unto themselves, in order to keep a game they feared away from an electorate they manipulate.

(The same can be said of the NAS officials who demand that the God hypothesis be censored in science classrooms. They act above the law. They don't care about the rights guaranteed by the First Amendment. Theirs is an anti-free speech, censorship mentality.)

You can read the details of our failed law cases at welfaregame.com. Lies of some of the defendants, and lies and manipulation of the law by some of their attorneys, and the bias of the judges kept us from getting either of two actions in front of a jury. Both cases were appealed to the U.S. Supreme Court, but our writs of certiorari were rejected.

Judges tend to favor establishment "experts," because they see themselves as part of the same class. Underlying the various decisions of the judges was the assumption that social engineering by the government involving massive welfare expenditures is a good thing, and that those who initiate and carry out expansive welfare policies are the good guys. I would argue that welfare empire "entitlements" have destroyed incentives to work, and created and perpetuated a crime-ridden, dependent underclass in the process.

By taking a pro-welfare point of view, the federal judges who heard our cases violated their own standards. The Supreme Court has stated firmly that this country has "a profound national commitment to the principle that debate on public issues should be uninhibited, robust and wide-open, and that it may include vehement, caustic and sometimes unpleasantly sharp attacks on government and public officials" (New York Times Co. v. Sullivan); that First Amendment freedoms are protected not only "against heavy-handed frontal attack, but also from being stifled by subtle governmental interference" (NAACP v. Alabama); the "evils to be prevented (are) not the censorship of the press, merely, but any action of government by means of which it might prevent such free and general discussion of public matters . . ." (Grossjean v. American Press Co.); "It is firmly settled that under our Constitution the public expression of ideas may not be prohibited merely because the ideas are themselves offensive to some of their hearers" (Bachellar v. Maryland); that the avoidance of censorship is to "preserve an uninhibited marketplace of ideas in which truth will ultimately prevail" (Red Lion Broadcasting Co. v. FCC); and that it is the duty of the government "to preserve inviolate the constitutional rights of free speech, free press and free assembly in order to maintain the opportunity for free political discussion, to the end that government may be responsive to the will of the people and that changes, if desired, may be obtained by peaceful means" (Dejonge v. Oregon).

One of the judges who denied one of our appeals himself had written that embedded in our democracy was the basic conviction that wisdom and justice are most likely to prevail in "public decision making if all ideas, discoveries, and points of view are before the citizenry for its consideration . . . (and that) we must remain profoundly skeptical of government claims that state action affecting expression can survive constitutional objection" (Thomas v. Board of Ed., Granville Cent. Sch. Dist.).

The judges had no business taking a position on the merits of the game. Only our right to distribute our political impressions in the form of a satirical board game should have been at issue. Whether the game has a "distasteful nature" or is "the most original game of the decade, if not the century," whether it "perpetuates outdated myths" or is an accurate lampoon of America's welfare system in action, is for the American people to decide. There ought to be no other censor in our democracy.

106

(Creationists and intelligent design proponents also run into the problem of the judges' embracing of overriding false assumptions in court cases. In ruling against creationists regarding the Louisiana Creation Act, the Supreme Court was upset that creationism rejects "the factual basis of evolution in its entirety," the judges of course assuming that evolution has a factual basis (Edwards v. Aguillard, 1987). The NAS's big lie technique—"evolution is a fact and all scientists believe it"—has been very effective. In the most recent case concerning evolution (Kitzmiller v. Dover Area School District, 2005), the judge embraced the same false assumption in ruling against intelligent design. In addition, much of his published opinion was cut and pasted directly from ACLU pleadings in the case.)

Could the U.S. Congress pass a constitutional law saying that, in the science classroom, a certain hypothesis—specifically, the God hypothesis—is forbidden? No, they could not. Yet, based on the situation in our public school classrooms today, such a menacing law may as well have already been passed. The effect is the same, and that's what matters. The God hypothesis, a valid scientific hypothesis, has been censored in our public school science classrooms by the evo-atheists of the NAS.

Let me give you a visual representation of what is really happening. While passing through Saigon during my tour as an infantry officer in Viet Nam, a Vietnamese newspaper caught my eye because of the white space on the front page where an article should have been. I soon learned that the South Vietnamese government censored every news article that put the government in a bad light, or even hinted at its rampant corruption. They censored the paper by pulling the offending articles off the paste-up boards before they shot the negatives and burned the plates. Every page had white space where an article should have been. The censorship could not have been more obvious.

Think about information on the subject of science as a newspaper being circulated in our public school science classrooms. Because of pseudo-intellectual intimidation from the NAS, on every page where there should be an enlightening and useful article, there is white space. Before long, writers with something important to say, but forbidden to say it, will stop writing. There won't be any more white space—not because there is no more censorship in the science classroom—but because the NAS censorship has triumphed. Students will not even realize that what they are being taught is the version censored by the goons from the NAS.

The hysterical rantings of the NAS propagandist Paul Henle blame the decline of science education in America on the "unwarranted" criticism of evo-atheism. The leaders of the NAS, with their outright contempt for free speech and free thought in the science classroom, are the true villains.

Chapter 9

THE FORBIDDEN THEORY OF ANCIENT GREEK ART

The cover of the February, 2008 issue of the *Smithsonian* featured a photograph of the Parthenon with the words "Secrets of the ancient temple." The nine-page article focused on the precision of construction. This has never been a secret, but rather something known since the time it was built on the Acropolis of Athens in the 5th century BC.

The structure, with all its precision, had three purposes that the *Smithsonian* barely touched upon: first, to make a covered space for the 40-foot-tall gold and ivory idol-image of Athena; second, to elevate the seven sculptural themes; and third, to make sure their messages to posterity as expressed in the sculptures survived as long as possible.

The evo-atheist editors at the *Smithsonian* accept academia's lame explanation that the sculptures depict "mythical themes," so they do not even question their real meaning or their relevance to us today. Is that what the Jefferson and Lincoln Memorials in our nation's capital depict, mythical themes? No, these monuments, these modern temples, say to the visitor, "Look at the historical foundations of our society. Look at the ideals we value and live by." The ancient Greeks, who created the living basis of our Western culture, expressed the same kind of sentiment to their own citizens and to posterity with their magnificent temples. But the art historians, the archaeologists, and the anthropologists who examine the Parthenon today cannot see it. The reason: evo-atheism rules those fields of study, and even when presented with the most obvious artistic depictions of Genesis events on the Parthenon, or in any other part of Greek art, they must be summarily denied and dismissed. The Genesis interpretation of Greek art is forbidden.

As we look at my forbidden theory of ancient Greek art in this chapter, we'll see specifically how the NAS's taboo against postulating a Creator works against the progress of understanding in the historical sciences, and against true scientific understanding in general.

Figs. 1, 2, and 3. Greek artists made certain there was no mistaking Athena's association with the serpent and its wisdom. Above left, from her pre-Parthenon temple, she wears a crown of serpents. In the vase-depiction below left, she wears the Gorgon Medusa, the head of serpents on her *aegis*, or goatskin. And as a part of her reconstructed idol-image in the Parthenon in Nashville, the ancient serpent rises up next to her as a friend. She holds Nike in her right hand: her friendship with the serpent has led her to Victory.

THE ORIGIN OF THE FORBIDDEN THEORY

I started thinking about ancient Greek art when I was a cadet at West Point. The helmet of Athena, goddess of war and wisdom, is the centerpiece of the academy crest which we wore for four years on our caps and shirt collars. Beginning with senior year, we carried the academy crest, with Athena's helmet, on our class rings. When I first saw a replica of Athena's Parthenon idol-image in the officers' club, I was most struck by the huge, friendly serpent rising up next to her. As a rule, women don't like serpents and men aren't crazy about them either. I remember thinking, "The Genesis serpent befriended Eve. Could this be the Genesis serpent?" Such was my speculation, based on something tangible and real in humanity's past. Scientific study begins with a question about something we observe, but don't yet understand.

Most mythology books refer to Athena as the goddess of wisdom, but as I looked deeper into her ancient idol-image and other depictions of her, I learned that the ancient artists made a point to associate her irrevocably with the serpent. On one sculpture, she wore a crown of serpents (fig. 1). This suggests that the serpent ruled her thinking. She was often depicted wearing a serpent-fringed *aegis*, or goat skin, as a symbol of her authority. On that aegis, she wore the Gorgon Medusa— the head of serpents (fig. 2). Was she, in truth, the goddess of the serpent's wisdom? The wisdom of the ancient serpent from Genesis?

From that point, I developed this working hypothesis: "Greek art depicts the early events described in Genesis, but from the standpoint that the serpent enlightened, rather than deluded, mankind." I called it the Genesis hypothesis. For my hypothesis to progress, I needed more factual connections. Did the Greeks speak of a first couple in an ancient paradise? Yes. You can examine the plentiful evidence for this, and for other connections between Genesis events and ancient Greek art in detail in my publications and at solvinglight.com. Let me here present a brief outline of what I have uncovered.

THE FIRST COUPLE

There is no Creator-God in the Greek religious system. Ancient Greek religion is about getting away from the God of Genesis, and exalting man as the measure of all things. You may think to yourself that the Greeks are exalting gods, not man; but haven't you ever wondered why the Greek gods looked exactly like humans? The answer is the obvious one: for the most part, the gods represented the Greeks' (and our) human ancestors. Greek religion was thus a sophisticated form of ancestor worship. In Plato's *Euthydemus*, Sokratres referred to Zeus, Athena, and Apollo as his "gods" and as his "lords and ancestors."[1] Greek stories about their origins are varied and sometimes contradictory until their poets and artists present Zeus and Hera as the couple from whom the other Olympian gods and mortal men are descended.

This brother/sister and husband/wife pair, the king and queen of the gods, are a match for the Adam and Eve of Genesis. This couple is the beginning of the family of man, and the origin of the family of the Greek gods, Zeus and Hera. With no Creator-God in the Greek religious system, the first couple advances to the forefront.

ZEUS AND HERA ARE THE FIRST COUPLE DESCRIBED IN GENESIS

According to the Book of Genesis, Eve is the mother of all humans, and the wife of Adam. Since God is the Father of both Adam and Eve, some consider them to be brother and sister as well. After they had both eaten the fruit, Adam named his wife Eve ("Living" in Hebrew) and Genesis 3:20 explains why: "... for she becomes the mother of all the living." In a hymn of invocation, the 6th-century BC lyric poet, Alcaeus, refers to Hera as "mother of all."[2] As the first wife, the Greeks worshipped Hera as the goddess of marriage; as the first mother, the Greeks worshipped her as the goddess of childbirth.

We are told in Chapter 2 of Genesis that Eve was created full-grown out of Adam. Before she was known as Hera, the wife of Zeus had the name *Dione*. The name relates to the creation of Eve out of Adam, for *Dione* is the feminine form of *Dios* or Zeus. This suggests that the two, like Adam and Eve, were once a single entity.

From the Judeo-Christian standpoint, the taking of the fruit by Eve and Adam at the serpent's behest was shameful, a transgression of God's commandment. From the Greek standpoint, however, the taking of the fruit was a triumphant and liberating act which brought to mankind the serpent's enlightenment. To the Greeks, the serpent was a friend of mankind who freed us from bondage to an oppressive God, and was therefore a savior and illuminator of our race.

In his *Works and Days*, the poet Hesiod wrote of "how the gods and mortal men sprang from one source."[3] The first couple, Zeus and Hera, were that source. Hera is the single mother of all humanity, and Zeus is, according to Hesiod, "the father of men and gods."[4] The term "father Zeus" is a description of the king of the gods which appears over 100 times in the ancient writings of Homer.[5] As the source of their history, Zeus and Hera became the gods of their history. Those without a belief in the Creator have only nature, themselves, and their progenitors to exalt.

The Greek tradition insists that Zeus and Hera were the first couple; the Judeo-Christian tradition insists Adam and Eve were the first couple. Two opposite spiritual standpoints share the same factual basis.

THE GREEK VERSION OF EDEN

If the above is true, then the Greeks ought to have directly connected Zeus and Hera to an ancient paradise, a serpent, and a fruit tree. They did, indeed, make such a direct connection.

The Greeks remembered the original paradise. They called it the Garden of the Hesperides, and they associated Zeus and Hera with its enticing ease, and with a serpent-entwined apple tree.

Some mythologists have mistaken the Hesperides for guardians of the tree, but they certainly are not. Their body language, their easy actions and their very names serve the purpose of establishing what kind of a garden this is: a wonderful, carefree place. In figure 4 (next page), we see the Garden of the Hesperides depicted on a water pot from about 410 BC. The serpent entwines the apple tree with its golden fruit. The names of the figures are written on the vase. Two of the Hesperides, *Chrysothemis* (Golden Order) and *Asterope* (Star Face) stand to the immediate left of the tree. Chrysothemis moves toward the tree to pluck an apple. Asterope leans pleasantly against her with both arms. To the left of them, *Hygeia* (Health) sits on a hillock and holds a long scepter, a symbol of rule, as she looks back towards the tree. To the right of the apple tree, *Lipara* (Shining Skin) holds apples in the fold of her garment, and raises her veil off her shoulder.

The names of the Hesperides describe what the garden is like. It is a land of gold for the taking, soft starlight, perfect health, and wondrous beauty. The Hebrew word for Eden means "to be soft or pleasant," figuratively "to delight oneself." The Garden of the Hesperides is the Greek version of the Garden of Eden.

**Figure 4: Vase-depiction of the Garden of the Hesperides,
the Greek version of Eden**

ZEUS AND HERA IN THE ANCIENT PARADISE

If Adam and Eve, in the Greek religious system, have become Zeus and Hera, there should be literary evidence for their presence in this garden, and there is. Apollodorus wrote that the apples of the Hesperides "were presented by Gaia [Earth] to Zeus after his marriage with Hera."[6] This matches the Genesis account: Eve became Adam's wife right after she was taken out of Adam (Genesis 2:21–25), and the next recorded event is the taking of the fruit by the first couple. Connecting Zeus and Hera with the Hesperides connects them with the serpent and the fruit tree with which the Hesperides are always represented.

The chorus in Euripides' play *Hippolytus* speaks of "the apple-bearing shore of the Hesperides" where immortal fountains flow "by the place where Zeus lay, and holy Earth with her gifts of blessedness makes the gods' prosperity wax great."[7] Thus Euripides put Zeus in the garden, and his language affirms that this is where Zeus came from.

You have probably heard one time or another about Eve eating the apple. The Hebrew word for fruit in Chapter 3 of Genesis is a general term. The idea that Adam and Eve took a bite of an apple comes to us as part of the Greek tradition.

Up to this point, we have developed a sound working hypothesis. The evidence is compelling. But we must remember, the ruling evo-

114

atheist paradigm is not about evidence, but rather, about validating their evo-atheist standpoint, and that's all. My line of thinking challenges their evo-atheist standpoint; therefore, it is forbidden. Evo-atheist writer Joseph Campbell, articulates the operative taboo as it applies to the fields of art history, Classical studies, archaeology, and anthropology today:

No one of adult mind today would turn to the Book of Genesis to learn of the origins of the earth, the plants, the beasts, and man. There was no flood, no tower of Babel, no first couple in paradise, and between the first known appearance of men on earth and the first building of cities, not one generation (Adam to Cain) but a good two million must have come into this world and passed along. Today we turn to science for our imagery of the past and of the structure of the world, and what the spinning demons of the atom and the galaxies of the telescope's eye reveal is a wonder that makes the babel of the Bible seem a toyland dream of the dear childhood of our brain.[8]

The Scriptures are false. Science is truth. Evolution is science. Evolution is truth. We've heard all of these atheistic assumptions before from the NAS. But where is the evidence that the Genesis events did not occur? And where is the evidence that evolution did occur? Campbell does not produce a shred of evidence to back up his speculation. Campbell's writings express the same profane prattlings, and the same philosophy and empty seduction we find in the NAS book. Genesis events must be explained away as fairy tales, and never examined as history; Greek art must be explained away as myth, and never examined as history—even though Genesis and Greek art corroborate each other. The truth is that Genesis *describes* the key events in early human history, while ancient Greek art *depicts* those same events, albeit from an opposite perspective. Let's see what else in ancient Greek art stares the evo-atheists in the face, but which they are forced to ignore and dismiss because of the narrow and limiting scope of their atheistic religious philosophy.

THE TWO ANTAGONISTIC SONS OF THE FIRST FAMILY

Now if Zeus and Hera are pictures of Adam and Eve, we would expect them to have two male children with antagonistic lines of descent just as the Genesis couple did. Zeus and Hera did have two male children: Hephaistos, the elder, and Ares; and they were as averse to each other as Kain (Cain) and Seth.

Adam and Eve actually had three sons: Kain, Abel and Seth, but Kain killed Abel before the latter had offspring. Greek artists knew all about that first murder. They depicted that event in a series of four metopes (square sculpted scenes) on the south side of the Parthenon (see Chapter 6 of *The Parthenon Code*). An explosion in 1687 destroyed the metopes, but fortunately, French artist, Jacques Carrey, had drawn them in 1674. You can see them at solvinglight.com. Classical scholars have no other cogent explanation for the four related scenes.

Since Seth replaced Abel, we look at Adam and Eve as having two sons, each of whom, in turn, had offspring. In the Scriptures, the line of Seth is the line of Christ. The Book of Matthew traces the lineage of Christ through David to Abraham; and the Book of Luke further traces the lineage of Abraham to Adam through his son Seth. This is often referred to as the line of belief in the Creator-God or the line of faith. On the other hand, the Scriptures define the line of Kain as one of unbelief in the Creator-God. According to I John 3:12, "Kain was of the wicked one," a reference to "the ancient serpent called Adversary and Satan, who is deceiving the whole inhabited earth" (Revelation 12:9).

The Greeks deified Kain as Hephaistos, god of the forge. They deified his younger brother, Seth, as Ares, the troublesome god of conflict and war. In the Judeo-Christian tradition, Kain is the evil one whose way is to be shunned. In the Greek religious system, Ares, the Seth of Genesis, is the traitor and the one who causes ruin and woe.

HEPHAISTOS/KAIN

By his Roman name, Vulcan, we associate Hephaistos, the deified Kain, immediately with the forge and the foundry. According to Genesis 4:22, the members of Kain's family were the first to become forgers "of every tool of copper and iron." These surely included the hammer, the axe, and the tongs—the tools most often associated with Hephaistos in Greek art.

Hephaistos' banishment from, and return to, Olympus (a place where the Creator is excluded from the pantheon) is a "myth" which constituted an essential element of Greek religion. It appeared painted, sculpted and bronzed throughout the Archaic and Classical periods. In the Greek religious system, the banishment and return of Hephaistos to Olympus corresponds, in Genesis, to Kain's being commanded to wander the earth by God, and his defiant return to establish the first city (Genesis 4:9-17).

ARES/SETH

Zeus loved his son Hephaistos, who performed an indispensable and appreciated function as armorer of the gods. On the other hand, Zeus considered his youngest son, Ares, to be worthless, calling him "hateful" and "pestilent" and a "renegade."[9] The ancient poet, Homer, referred to Ares as "the bane of mortals."[10] The only reason Ares has a place in the Greek pantheon is that he is the son of Zeus; that is, he is one of the two actual sons of the first couple, Adam and Eve, of whom Zeus and Hera are deifications. Zeus hates Ares, but accepts responsibility for siring him: "[F]or thou art mine offspring, and it was to me that thy mother bare thee," and then rails at this son of his, telling him that if he were born of any other god, he would have been "lower than the sons of heaven" long ago.[11] Some scholars say Greek religion is anthropomorphic; that is, gods take human form. That's not quite right. What happens is that real human ancestors retain their original identities and take on godlike qualities. Ares, as a deification of Seth, is trapped by the historical framework. His father, Zeus, had to hate him, and the Greek hero, Herakles, was expected to kill Ares' children.

While the scriptural viewpoint defines Seth/Ares as the God-believing, or spiritual son, Greek religion defines him as hated by, and antagonistic to, the ruling gods who are part of the serpent's system. Likewise, while Zeus-religion looks on Hephaistos/Kain as the true and devoted son, the scriptural viewpoint defines him as part of the wicked one's system. Jews and Christians dislike and shun the line of Kain, but they can't get rid of him or his line without altering their spiritual standpoint and history itself. Kain is part of the Scriptures, and he is there to stay. Zeus-religion has the same kind of situation. It hates the line of Ares, but it cannot eliminate the line from its history because the basic achievement of Zeus-religion, its grand celebration even, is the triumph of the way of Kain over the way of Seth. Ares is part of Greek sacred literature and art, and he is there to stay.

THE GREEK DEPICTION OF THE FLOOD

According to Genesis, the Flood temporarily wiped out the way of Kain. Noah, in the line of Seth, "a just man" (Genesis 6:9), survived with his wife, three sons, and their wives in the ark. All but these eight people disappeared into the earth. The Greeks pictured this cataclysmic event as half-men/half-horses known as Kentaurs (Centaurs) pounding a man named Kaineus into the ground (fig.5). Kaineus means "pertaining to Kain," or more directly, "the line of Kain."

Who were the Kentaurs? The original Greek word for Kentaur, *Kentauros*, means hundred (where we get century and cent) and most likely relates to the fact that Noah, the chief of the line of Seth, warned of the Flood for one hundred years.[12] In most vase paintings of them, the Kentaurs carried symmetrical branches, a sign that they belonged to a certain branch of humanity. The Greeks, who embraced the way of Kain, did not acknowledge the Creator God, and so they couldn't blame Him for the Flood. They blamed the survivors of it, that strange branch of humanity they didn't really understand—the line of Seth.

The evo-atheists have no explanation for the connection between Kain and Hephaistos and Seth and Ares, nor do they have an explanation for Kaineus and the Kentaurs. Because ignorant atheists say so, entire fields of scientific enquiry must arbitrarily dismiss the only real evidence we have for the origin of mankind.

Figs. 5 and 6. Left, Kaineus (the line of Kain) disappears into the earth during the Flood at the hands of the Seth-men (Kentaurs). Right, after the Flood, Athena welcomes the reborn line of Kain (the child is the seed of Hephaistos/Kain) from the earth in Athens.

Let's see what else the evo-atheists scholars and their spell-bound students are forced to ignore in the ancient Greek record.

THE RESURGENCE OF THE WAY OF KAIN AFTER THE FLOOD

For a number of years after the Flood, God's awesome and decisive intervention in human affairs remained fresh in the minds of Noah's descendants, and the way of Kain remained dormant. Then, gradually, a yearning for a return to the serpent's wisdom began to take hold.

The evidence I present in my books and in my 950-slide PowerPoint presentation shows irrefutably that Greek religious art celebrated the resurgence and victory of the way of Kain after the Flood. The question is, how did the way of Kain come through the Flood? The answer is, through a woman. The evidence for this is found in an extremely well-researched 782-page book by Anne Baring and Jules Cashford called *The Myth of the Goddess*. The authors trace the goddesses of the ancient Near-eastern and Mediterranean world to a single original goddess named Nammu.

"The earliest Sumerian creation myth," they write, "tells the story of Nammu, Goddess of the Primordial Waters, who brought forth the cosmic mountain, An-Ki, Heaven and Earth."[13] The Primordial Waters are the Flood waters; the cosmic mountain, where the ark landed. The

119

peaks of the mountains of Ararat often disappeared into the clouds, so it seemed Nammu had come from above, from heaven to earth.

Most of the significant ancient goddesses were linked to the Flood in some way, beginning with the one whom they represented, Nammu. Baring and Cashford: "The images of water and sea, the unfathomable abyss of the Deep, return us to Nammu, the Sumerian goddess whose ideogram was the sea . . ."[14] Baring and Cashford again: "Asherah [a Caananite goddess] was called 'the Lady of the Sea,' which links her to the Sumerian Nammu, and to the Egyptian Isis, 'born in all wetness.'"[15] Those descriptions of the goddess evoke the memory of the Flood. But where did Nammu come from? Baring and Cashford do not know.

Operating in the academic world under the evo-atheist paradigm, the authors cannot make the obvious Genesis connection. Genesis 4:17-22 records the descendents of Kain beginning with his son, Enoch, going down to his great-great-great-great grandson, Tubal-kain. The writer of Genesis pens one more sentence at the end of the male line of Kain: "And the sister of Tubal-kain is Naamah" (Genesis 4:22). The line of Seth (Genesis 5:6-32) mentions no women. Why is Naamah mentioned in the line of Kain?

My answer, as expressed in Section I of *Noah in Ancient Greek Art*, is that Noah's son, Ham, married her, and brought her with him on the ark through the Flood. After the Flood, Naamah/Nammu reverted to the way of Kain, and instigated the rebellion which the Greeks, as well as other nations, celebrated.

The Greeks recognized Ham as the friendly Kentaur, Chiron. Other Kentaurs of the line of Seth were enemies of the resurgent line of Kain, but not Chiron. Although he was a son of Noah, Ham connected with the line of Kain through his marriage to the Kain-woman, Naamah/Nammu. Greek artists honored him for bringing her through the Flood, and depicted him in a radically different way from all the other Kentaurs. He is not pictured as a crude enemy, but as a civilized friend. His front legs are not equine, but human. If you stood directly in front of him, you wouldn't even know that he was a Kentaur. They called him Chiron because it means "hand" in Greek, and suggests that he gave an early helping hand to the development of Zeus-religion.

On the following page, we see how the Greeks depicted and named Noah, his son Ham, his grandson, Cush, and his great-grandson, Nimrod. In *The Parthenon Code* and *Noah in Ancient Greek Art*, I present detailed evidence which connects these ancient historical figures.

Over several generations, Naamah, with the help of her son and grandson, Cush and Nimrod, won the adoration of the majority of humanity, taking credit for bringing civilization through the Flood. As the tribes and nations began to form, they worshipped different aspects of Naamah using different names.

Figure 7. An ancient depiction shows Herakles shoving Nereus aside. Nereus means the "Wet One." The Greeks also referred to him as the "Salt Sea Old Man." He is the Greek version of Noah. Herakles is the Nimrod of Genesis, the grandson of Naamah. He led mankind's rebellion after the Flood with her as his guide.

I would change the title of Baring's and Cashford's book from *The Myth of the Goddess* to *The Memory of the Adored Woman*, because that's what it is really all about. The authors cannot see this simple truth, and so remain puzzled as to why ancient goddesses so dominated ancient Mediterranean cultures: Ishtar, Inanna, Asherah, Isis, Demeter, Artemis, Athena—all, in their own scholarly judgment, derived from Nammu. Baring and Cashford confess that they do not know how the goddess image first arose, "whether from dreaming sleep or from waking vision." But it was not a dream or a vision that led to the veneration of the goddess throughout the ancient world, but rather a real woman named Naamah, the last person mentioned in the line of Kain before the

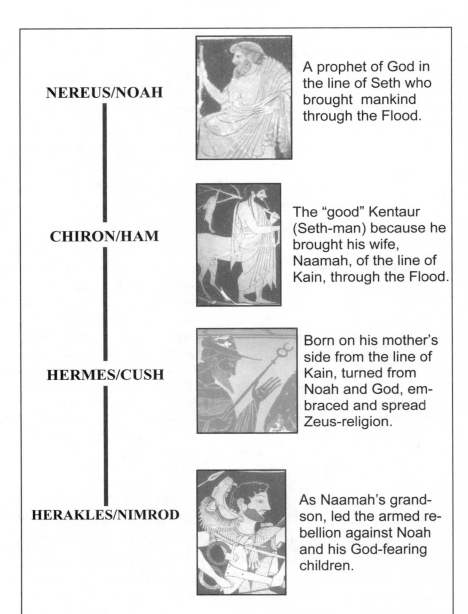

NEREUS/NOAH

A prophet of God in the line of Seth who brought mankind through the Flood.

CHIRON/HAM

The "good" Kentaur (Seth-man) because he brought his wife, Naamah, of the line of Kain, through the Flood.

HERMES/CUSH

Born on his mother's side from the line of Kain, turned from Noah and God, embraced and spread Zeus-religion.

HERAKLES/NIMROD

As Naamah's grandson, led the armed rebellion against Noah and his God-fearing children.

Figure 8. Here is how the renunciation of Noah and his God proceeded from his son, Ham (who brought Naamah through the Flood as his wife) through his son, Cush, to his son, Nimrod. Or as the Greeks remembered them, from Chiron through Hermes to Herakles. The most influential person in this great spiritual transformation, Ham's wife Naamah/Athena, is not shown here.

Flood. The majority of humanity adored her because she brought the way of Kain through the Flood, and through her offspring, Cush/ Hermes and Nimrod/Herakles, reestablished its dominance.

If, in the Greek religious system, Demeter, Artemis, and Athena are all personas or aspects of the real woman, Naamah/Nammu, why is Athena the dominant one? Why is she the favored daughter of Zeus? It is because Athena represents the most essential aspect of Naamah— dedication and submission to the ancient serpent and its wisdom. That is the heart and soul of Zeus-religion and the way of Kain. As Naamah/ Demeter, the goddess of vegetation, she brought the seeds through the Flood; as Naamah/Artemis, the mistress of wild beasts, she brought the animals through the Flood. Both were very important, but it is the exaltation of the serpent's wisdom that is the distinguishing, defining, and crucial achievement of Naamah/Athena. Only two ancestors are ever depicted in Greek art holding Nike, or Victory, in their hand. One is Adam/Zeus, the original purveyor to humanity of the serpent's wisdom before the Flood. The other is Naamah/Athena, the woman who brought back the serpent's enlightenment to mankind after the Flood. That is why Greek artists almost always depicted Athena with a serpent or serpents. That is why Athena's temple stood in all its glory above the city of Athens. That is the secret of the Parthenon.

Naamah/Athena's grandson, Nimrod/Herakles became the great hero who supplied the muscle to overthrow Noah/Nereus and his God-fearing offspring. At solvinglight.com, I present 37 images of Noah from ancient Greek art. In almost all the scenes, the patriarch's authority is being usurped by the rebel, Nimrod/Herakles, or he is being forced by the artists to witness key events leading to the triumph of Zeus-religion. Noah/Nereus is a benchmark figure. Artists placed him in scenes as the known character, the constant against which they could portray the great spiritual/religious change taking place after the Flood.

Also at solvinglight.com, we restore the 12 labors of Herakles in color, as they originally appeared on the temple of Zeus at Olympia. Once you examine the images of Noah, the labors of Herakles, and the restoration of the east pediment of the Parthenon, with their respective explanations on the Web site, I think you will agree that the Genesis

Figs. 9 and 10. From opposite sides of the same vase, Cush/Hermes, with Nimrod/Herakles in his arms, runs away from his father, a bewildered, Ham/Chiron. Hermes has sided with his mother, Naamah/Athena of the line of Kain. Naamah/Athena inspired and led her grandson, Nimrod/Herakles, in his labors and other exploits.

Figs. 11 and 12. The sculpted scenes above the east entrance of the temple of Zeus at Olympia, restored by Holmes Bryant. Left, Herakles kills the three-bodied Geryon, symbolizing the authority of the three sons of Noah. Right, with Noah's sons overcome, and with Athena's help, Herakles pushes away the heavens, and with them, the God of the heavens, enabling the strong man to retrieve from Atlas the golden apples from the ancient serpent's tree.

124

hypothesis of Greek art has become an authentic theory. I go so far as to consider it fact, but I leave that determination up to you.

Herakles' labors chronicle and celebrate mankind's successful rebellion against Noah and his God after the Flood. The Greek hero's labors and battles were directed toward one goal: getting back to the serpent's enlightenment in the ancient garden, as symbolized by possession of the apples from its tree (figs. 11 and 12). Of course, Herakles did not really get back to the ancient garden; it is a figurative artistic statement: the Greeks will not live under Noah and his God any longer, but will re-embrace the "enlightenment" of the ancient serpent, and live by the fruit of its tree. Zeus-religion celebrates the great change in the post-Flood religious paradigm. Noah and his God are out. The serpent and its enlightenment are back in. Humanity has decided this: mankind is now the measure of all things.

This is exactly what the evo-atheists believe. This is the sentiment Zimmerman and Mr. X express in their Clergy Project Letter. The members of the hierarchy of the NAS go a step further than exalting mankind as the measure of all things. They exalt *themselves* as the measure of all things. They redefine science to accord with their atheism. They decide what our children will be taught about their origins. They determine which thoughts are mandatory in the science classroom, and which are impermissible. They insist that their atheistic philosophy and religion be honored as supreme.

Do the evo-atheists understand the meaning of Greek art in general or the Parthenon sculptures in particular? No. This is one of the great ironies of our time. The evo-atheists at the NAS, the editors at the *Smithsonian*, the thousands of other evo-atheist media chieftains, and the evo-atheists throughout academia do not recognize *their own* humanistic belief system as it appears glorified in ancient Greek sculpture and vase-painting. They are blind to it. In their enchanted state of cognitive obliviousness, it doesn't matter to them.

In all my research, I have never encountered a sound theory of Greek art, other than the one presented here. That is because nothing but the Genesis theory fits the facts. After the Flood, the Greeks rebelled against Noah and his God, preferring to idolize their human forebears in the way of Kain who had reestablished and systematized their man-centered religious outlook. It is as simple and as obvious as that.

Modern academia has yet to learn the simple lesson that, without reference to the early events described in the Book of Genesis, it is not possible to make any real sense of ancient Greek art and religion. In fact, the entire formidable religious framework of ancient Greek society means virtually nothing without reference to those events. The problem for these academics is that they cannot entertain the Genesis theory of Greek art without abandoning, or at least seriously questioning, their own evo-atheism. The evo-atheist taboo forbids them to explore a rich world of deep intellectual (in the best sense of the term) stimulation and understanding. They are called teachers and professors, yet they fail to comprehend the meaning of the symbolic art that our ancient ancestors have left for us, just as they fail to recognize the handiwork of our Creator throughout the earth, and within all the life upon it.

Atheism leads nowhere. It is nothing more than an outright denial of what is intuitively apparent. Atheists have taken over the National Academy of Sciences. With God pushed out of the picture, they need to concoct an alternative explanation for our existence. That's all molecules-to-man evolution is—a concocted rationale for atheism.

Today, those working in the historical sciences who want their careers to progress must rigidly follow the evo-atheist paradigm of the NAS. Mainstream archaeologists hardly think about Genesis. The NAS insists that mainstream anthropologists study chimpanzees, while ridiculing those who dare to examine with open minds the true record of our origins found in ancient art and literature.

Look what the NAS atheists have done to science in order to justify their own unbelief in God. To them, science is not an open-ended search for truth. Beginning with their denial of the obvious, they have made science into the manipulation of language, the philosophical contamination of nature, and the fabrication of evidence to validate the atheism of the NAS hierarchy.

Their illogic and their seductions cannot bear the salutary tonics of open debate and free inquiry. The NAS atheists detest the valid God hypothesis and the proven (in my opinion) theory of the meaning of ancient Greek art. They cannot disprove these ideas, so they must intimidate those who are inclined to consider them. Brandishing a club as dangerous as the one wielded by Herakles, the NAS hierarchy threatens us, spiritually attacking our children and our way of life in a most serious and sinister way. It is time to call them to account for the evil they have done, and are doing, in the name of "science."

NOTES

CHAPTER 1

1. Julian Huxley, *Essays of a Humanist* (New York: Harper and Row, 1964), p.125.
2. Provine, Will, "No Free Will," in *Catching Up with the Vision*, ed. by Margaret W. Rossister (Chicago: University of Chicago Press, 1999), p. S123. Thanks for citations 1 and 2 to Henry M. Morris in 'The Scientific Case Against Evolution," icr.org.
3. Richard Dawkins, "Put Your Money on Evolution," *The New York Times* (April 9, 1989), section VII, p. 35.
4. Law, Stephen, "Is Creationism Scientific," in *Darwin Day Collection One*, ed. by Amanda Chesworth, et. al (Albuquerque: Tangled Ban Press, 2002), p. 291.

CHAPTER 2

1. *Unlocking the Mystery of Life: The Scientific Case for Intelligent Design*, DVD/VHS, Illustra Media, 2002.

CHAPTER 3

1. Peter Hastie, *Creation Magazine*, Sep.-Nov. 1995, Vol. 17, No. 4, pp. 14-16. Creation Ministries International.
2. Niles Eldredge, as quoted in: Luther D. Sunderland, *Darwin's Enigma: Fossils and Other Problems*, fourth edition (revised and expanded), Master Book Publishers, Santee (California),1988, p. 78.
3. Scienceagainstevolution.org/v7i1n.htm
4. Feduccia, A.; in: V. Morell, "Archaeopteryx: Early Bird Catches a Can of Worms," Science 259 (5096):764–65, 5 February 1993.

CHAPTER 4

1. Henry M. Morris, "The Scientific Case Against Evolution," Institute for Creation Research, icr.org, p.4.

CHAPTER 6

1. Ruse M., *Darwinism Defended: A Guide to the Evolution Controversies* Addison-Wesley: Reading MA, 1983, Third Printing, p. 280.
2. Kofman, Sarah, *Socrates: Fictions of a Philosopher*, Cornell University Press, 1998, p. 203.

CHAPTER 7

1. Lynn Margulis and Dorion Sagan, *Acquiring Genomes: A Theory of the Origins of the Species*, (Basic Books, 2003), p. 29.

CHAPTER 9

1. Plato, Euthydemus, from: *The Dialogues of Plato*, Jowett, B. (Translator), Third Edition, Vol. I, Oxford at the Clarendon Press: Oxford University Press, Humphrey Milford Publisher, 1892, 302d.
2. Hornblower, S. and Spawforth, A. (Eds.), *The Oxford Companion to Classical Civilization*, Oxford University Press, Oxford and New York, 1998, p. 332.
3. Hesiod, *Works and Days*, Evelyn-White, H.G. (Translator), William Heinemann Ltd and Harvard University Press, London, 1914, 105.
4. Hesiod, Ref. 3, 59.
5. Homer, *The Iliad*, Lattimore, R. (Translator), University of Chicago Press, Lattimore, R. (Translator), University of Chicago Press, Iliad Chicago and London, 1961, 503 and frequently.
6. Apollodorus, *Apollodorus, The Library*, with an English Translation by Sir James George Frazer, 2 Volumes, Harvard University Press, Cambridge, Mass. and London, 1921, 2.5.11.
7. Euripides, *Hippolytus*, Kovacs, D. (Translator), Harvard University Press, Cambridge,1996 , 744–750.
8. Campbell, Joseph, *The Masks of God: Occidental Mythology*. The Viking Press, Inc., New York, 1964, p. 520.
9. Homer, Ref. 5, 885–889.
10. Homer, Ref. 5, 846.
11. Homer, Ref. 5, 895.
12. See 2 Peter 2:5; Genesis 5:32 and 7:6.
13. Baring, Anne and Cashford, Jules, *The Myth of the Goddess*, Arkana Penguin Books, London, 1993, p. 152.
14. Ibid., p.473.
15. Ibid., p.454.